PRAYING
through Life's
PROBLEMS

PRAYING
through Life's
PROBLEMS

featuring

STORMIE OMARTIAN,

JONI EARECKSON TADA, LESLIE VERNICK,
CATHERINE HART WEBER,
JOSEPH AND MARY ANN MAYO,
LINDA S. MINTLE *and* DIANE LANGBERG

INTEGRITY®
PUBLISHERS
Nashville

Praying through Life's Problems

Copyright © 2003 by American Association of Christian Counselors. All rights reserved.

Published by Integrity Publishers, a division of Integrity Media, Inc., 5250 Virginia Way, Suite 110, Brentwood, TN 37027 in association with American Association of Christian Counselors.

HELPING PEOPLE WORLDWIDE EXPERIENCE *the* MANIFEST PRESENCE *of* GOD.

Published in association with Yates and Yates, LLP, Literary Agents, Orange, California.

Unless otherwise indicated, Scripture quotations are taken from the Holy Bible, New International Version (NIV). Copyright © 1973, 1978, 1984 International Bible Society. Used by permission of Zondervan Bible Publishers.

Other Scripture quotations are from the following sources:

The American Standard Version (ASV), © copyright 1901. Public domain.

The New King James Version (NKJV), copyright © 1979, 1980, 1982, Thomas Nelson, Inc., Publishers.

New American Standard Bible (NASB) © 1960, 1977 by the Lockman Foundation.

Library of Congress Cataloging-in-Publication Data

Praying through life's problems / by Stormie Omartian . . . [et al].
    p. cm.
    ISBN 1-59145-057-8
    1. Christian women—Religious life. 2. Prayer—Christianity.
        I. Omartian, Stormie
BV4527.P68 2003
248.8'6—dc21

2003004721

Printed in the United States of America
03 04 05 06 07 08 RRD 9 8 7 6 5 4 3 2

Contents

Acknowledgments

The publishers wish to thank Tim Clinton and Doris Rikkers for their creative and editorial contributions to this project.

Introduction

Do not be anxious about anything,
but in everything, by prayer and petition,
with thanksgiving, present your requests to God.
And the peace of God, which transcends all understanding,
will guard your hearts and your minds in Christ Jesus.
—PHILIPPIANS 4:6–7

Life is full of difficulties, whether we suffer them ourselves or empathize in the suffering and difficulties of others. God has created us as caring and loving women who hurt deeply and feel deeply. God never intended life to be easy. If it were, we would not yearn for a better place—at His side in heaven, where we truly belong and where He wants us to be. But God has made us many promises: He will stand beside us no matter what we face, He will give us the strength to face each new day, and above all, He will listen to and answer our prayers, our cries for help.

In our most wrenching moments, in our times of pain and anger, depression and guilt, fear and hopelessness, we can crawl into the arms of Jesus and talk to Him. He has promised us that if we ask, we will receive. So when life is at its worst and you don't know how to endure one more moment, turn to Jesus—He is your source of comfort and hope.

Praying through Life's Problems

STORMIE OMARTIAN

> *Hear my prayer, O LORD;*
> *listen to my cry for mercy.*
> *In the day of my trouble I will call to you,*
> *for you will answer me.*
>
> —PSALM 86:6–7

Is there anyone in the world who never goes through difficult times? If so, I would like to meet that person. I just want to find out what that's like. I have known and walked with the Lord for over thirty-two years and I still go through difficult times, just like everyone else. But the longer I walk with God, the less discouraged and frightened I get by the troubling things that happen. I don't become hopeless like I used to. That's because I know God is in control of my life, and my hope is in Him. I pray to Him many times a day to make sure He and I stay in close touch, and I remind Him that I can't live without Him so He needs to be in charge of my life.

No matter how dark, disturbing, painful, and upsetting our circumstances may seem, there is a place of peace God has for each of us.

Don't get me wrong, I'm not saying that I am never taken by surprise when difficult situations occur. My initial reaction is not always perfect peace. Too often I get pulled headfirst into the mire of grief, pain, and despair over the things that happen to me and around me. Just when I think I have heard and seen it all, I find myself shocked at the new degrees of the unthinkable that the devil thinks up to destroy us. I can get horrified or afraid or even temporarily succumb to thinking that my life is over. But I soon come to my senses and realize that no matter how dark, disturbing, painful, and upsetting our circumstances may seem, there is a place of peace God has for each of us as a shelter from the storm. And we can depend on Him to take us there when we look to Him for refuge.

One of the best illustrations of this is whenever we take off in an airplane on a gray, dreary, rainy day. It's amazing how we can fly right up through the dark, wet clouds—so thick that we can't see one thing out the window—and then suddenly we rise above it all and have the ability to see for miles. Up there the sky is sunny, clear, and blue. I keep forgetting that no matter how bad the weather gets, it's possible to rise above the dark and gloom of the storm to a place where everything is fine.

Our spiritual and emotional lives are similar to that. When the dark clouds of trial, struggle, grief, or suffering roll in and settle on us so thick that we can barely see ahead of us, it's easy to forget that there is a place of calm, light, clarity, and peace we can rise to. If we take God's hand in those difficult times, He will lift us up above our circumstances to the place of comfort, warmth, and safety He has for us. Too often, though, we forget to take God's hand. We forget to walk with Him. We lose the understanding that our hope and comfort can only be found in Him.

One of my favorite names for the Holy Spirit is the Comforter (John 14:26 ASV). That name alone brings healing to our hearts. God loved us enough not to leave us here on earth to fend for ourselves, so He gave us the gift of His Holy Spirit. Just as we don't have to beg the sun for light, we don't have to beg the Holy Spirit for comfort. He *is* comfort. We simply have to separate ourselves from anything that separates us from Him and move into His presence. We have to pray that when we go through difficult times, He will give us an even greater sense of His presence as we endure.

Tough times happen to everyone. This last year and a half has been one of the most difficult periods in my life. While so many good things were happening to me in terms of God's blessings on my writing, I still had to fight for my life in the area of my physical health. About two years ago I started having attacks of severe abdominal pain and nausea. Every time one happened, it was unbearable and my husband would have to take me to the emergency hospital in the middle of the night. (Why is it always in the middle of the night?) We would end up being there until sometime the following day as doctors and technicians conducted every possible test to find the cause of my problem. But each test came back indicating that I was as healthy as I could possibly be. They could not find anything wrong with me, and no one could understand why I was suffering so much. This went on for six months as I was in and out of different hospitals, seeing different doctors and specialists.

Then in the middle of the most awful night I have ever experienced in my life, I felt something explode in my body so violently that I knew I would die if I didn't get help. My husband rushed me to the hospital at 3:30 in the morning because we knew I didn't have time to wait for an ambulance. But then I laid in the emergency room for hours begging someone to help me and telling people I was going to die if somebody didn't do something soon. I was given all the same tests they had given me many times before, and still no one could find anything wrong.

My husband prayed for me continually, and when my sister, Susan, and close friend, Roz, arrived, they prayed for me, too. They called other people to pray that someone would figure out what was wrong with me and do something. All I could pray was, "Help me, Jesus."

At one point I said to God, "Is this my time to die?" But I did not sense God saying that it was. In fact, I felt Him say that He still had things for me to do on earth. I felt encouraged by that, but the excruciating pain never let up and the medical staff could not give me anything for it until they knew exactly what was wrong. I kept praying for God to lift me to that place above the storm.

Finally, after eight hours of waiting in the emergency room, the specialist called in a surgeon who was brave enough to say, "I can't tell what is wrong with you by any of the tests, but I believe your appendix has ruptured. I'm going to take you into surgery immediately, and if I'm wrong I'll find out what the problem is." I thanked him profusely and told him to do whatever was necessary to stop the pain. I didn't care what he had to cut out as long as I didn't have to suffer this excruciating pain anymore. As it turned out, the surgeon was right. After the surgery when I was awake enough to talk, he told me, "In another hour you would have gone into a toxic-shock coma, and I could not have saved your life." I knew

God had answered our prayers for healing, and this doctor was an important part of that answer.

The battle was not over, however. For the next two weeks, I was hooked up to tubes and a machine and endured pain that made childbirth seem pleasant. Even constant morphine didn't take away all the pain or even make it bearable since the footlong incision in my abdomen had to be left as an open wound so the doctors could enter my abdomen every day to clean it out. I was still at risk, even after the surgery. As it turned out the doctor *never* sewed it up; instead he let the wound heal from the inside out—a process that took over five months. When I finally went home from the hospital, a nurse treated me seven days a week for many weeks. But within months, even before this first surgery was half-healed, I was back in the hospital for surgery again to have my gall bladder removed. The doctors finally determined that my gall bladder had been the cause of my abdominal pain in the first place.

During those eighteen months, I lived with excruciating emotional and physical pain. But I never doubted that God was in charge of my life. Did I feel fear? Yes. Did I get depressed? Sometimes. Did I not have enough faith? Probably. (When do we ever have enough faith?) Did this mean I was a failure? No, it just meant I was human and I have physical limitations like all people do. The enemy wanted me dead but God's grace and the prayers of many people kept Satan's plans from succeeding.

Now I ask you, does this story sound like the kind of thing that should be happening to someone who prays a lot? To someone who is serving the Lord the best she knows how? Is this the way things should go for a person whose life has never been easy? Actually, I'm beginning to think the answer to those questions is yes. That's because pain and loss are a part of life. We all suffer in some way at some time, especially if we are effectively serving the Lord. But the good news is that God is always there to bring good out of it when we invite Him to do so. When we walk with the Lord, our suffering is never in vain.

GOD'S REASONS FOR SUFFERING

There are different reasons that tough times happen, and if we can gain an understanding of the reason for our suffering, it will help us overcome our pain, rise to a place of peace, and see our faith grow in the midst of it.

1. *Sometimes difficult things happen to us so that the glory and power of God can be revealed in and through us.* Jesus passed by a man who was born blind and His disciples asked Him if his blindness was because the man's parents had sinned or he had sinned. Jesus replied, "Neither this man nor his parents sinned, but that the works of God should be revealed in him" (John 9:3 NKJV). We may not be able to understand why certain things are happening at the time, and we may never know the whole story until we go to be with the Lord, but when we turn to God in the midst of these difficult situations, God's glory will be seen in them. In my situation, God's glory was seen in the fact that I lived and did not die. It was seen in the powerful answers to prayer.

2. *Sometimes God uses difficult times to purify us.* The Bible says, "Since Christ suffered for us in the flesh, arm yourselves also with the same mind, for he who has suffered in the flesh has ceased from sin" (1 Peter 4:1 NKJV). This means our suffering during those particular times will burn sin and selfishness out of our lives. God allows suffering to happen so that

we will learn to live for Him and not for ourselves and that we will pursue His will and not our own. Suffering is never pleasant at the time, but God permits it so "that we may be partakers of His holiness" (Hebrews 12:10). He wants us to let go of the things we lust after and cling to what is most important in life—Him. When I was in that hospital bed in excruciating pain and unable to move without help, I was clinging to the Lord every moment for every breath. That's about as pure a life as you can get.

3. *Sometimes our misery is caused by God disciplining us.* "No chastening seems to be joyful for the present, but painful; nevertheless, afterward it yields the peaceable fruit of righteousness to those who have been trained by it" (Hebrews 12:11). The fruit that this godly disciplining and pruning produces in us is worth the trouble we have to go through to get it, even though it doesn't seem like it at the time. We have to be careful not to resist it or hate it. "Do not despise the chastening of the Lord, nor be discouraged when you are rebuked by Him; for whom the Lord loves He chastens, and scourges every son whom He receives" (Hebrews 12:5–6). I believe God was disciplining me in that season of

suffering by letting me see my own mortality up-close and showing me how short my time on earth is. He did that because He wanted me to let go of certain *good* things and devote myself to His *best* things.

4. *Sometimes we are caught in the midst of the enemy's work.* The enemy would like nothing more than to make you miserable and destroy your life. Often the reason for the anguish, sorrow, sadness, grief, or pain you feel entirely is Satan's doing and no fault of your own or anyone else's. Your comfort is in knowing that as you praise God in the midst of the attack upon you, He will defeat the enemy and bring good out of it that you can't even fathom. God wants you to walk with Him in faith as He leads you through suffering, so He can teach you to trust Him in the midst of it. God clearly showed my husband and me that Satan's plan was to destroy my life during my painful months of illness and recovery.

How to Pray in Difficult Times

Regardless of the reason for your difficulty, your prayers will make a positive difference on the outcome. Every day you have another opportunity to affect your future with the words you speak to God. Don't worry about how many times you feel you are praying the same prayer over and over; God

Regardless of the reason for your difficulty, your prayers will make a positive difference on the outcome.

freshly hears your words spoken to Him each time. Your prayer has new life every time you pray it. Even if you don't see answers to your prayers right away, each prayer sets something in motion. There is so much happening in the spirit realm that you don't see. Along with telling God your specific needs, here are some other ways to pray that will help you get through the difficult times:

1. *Pray for wisdom.* Whenever we don't make good choices in our lives, there is a price to pay. And we are never more in danger of making wrong decisions than when we are stressed, in pain, or suffering in some way. During those times it's easy to make a decision born out of desperation, so it's always good to ask God for wisdom and discernment. And this needs to be an ongoing prayer because too often we have to make quick decisions. On those occasions we

don't have time to seek the will of God. We need to already know it.

2. *Pray for the Holy Spirit's help.* When we're in the midst of tragedy, loss, devastation, or disappointment, we hurt terribly and find it impossible to think beyond the pain. But we don't have to go through those difficult times alone, because the Holy Spirit is there to help us. In some translations of the Bible, the Spirit is called the Helper. Jesus said, "I will pray the Father, and He will give you another Helper, that He may abide with you forever; the Spirit of truth" (John 14:16–17). When we turn to Him for help and comfort, we will find it. He will give us revelation and power, the very things we need most when we are struggling.

3. *Pray to have the mind of Christ.* The Bible says you "have the mind of Christ" (1 Corinthians 2:16), and you are to "let this mind be in you which was also in Christ Jesus" (Philippians 2:5). It also says, "since Christ suffered for you in the flesh, arm yourselves also with the same mind, for he who has suffered in the flesh has ceased from sin" (1 Peter 4:1). If you ask God to help you arm yourself with the mind of Christ, He will enable you to endure the suffering for the

glory set before you. In other words, He will help you focus on the good that He will bring out of the situation instead of the misery you are experiencing.

4. *Pray for a greater sense of God's presence.* In times of grief, suffering, or trial, ask God to help you sense His presence in a stronger way every day. Feeling God's presence around you will help you increase your faith and not be overcome with doubt; it will give you strength to stand strong in God's truth and not be swept away by your emotions or lies of the enemy; it will help you be content in your current situation because *He* is there. We all want to come to the place where we don't have to be afraid of bad news because our heart is steadfast, trusting in Him (Psalm 112:7). We want to sense the presence of the one who delivers our soul from death, and our eyes from tears, and our feet from falling (Psalm 116:8). We want to say, "I will not be afraid, because I know the Lord is with me." When you sense God's presence, it takes away your fear and gives you hope.

5. *Pray that you will stay in God's Word and obey it.* When the storm is raging around you, you want to be hanging onto something solid and unmovable. Nothing is more solid

than the Word of God. When I was sick I was so incapacitated that I couldn't even hold a Bible, so I had to depend on others to read it to me. Hearing God's Word lifted my spirits and strengthened me. It spoke of God's promises to me and gave me hope. It made me feel that everything was going to be all right. It will do that and more for you.

6. *Pray to see the good in bad things that happen.* None of us likes pain, uncertainty, strife, or frustration. We want things the way we want them. But the challenging and miserable times are not without their aspect of good. There are things that happen to us in those times that are as precious as diamonds. It's during the difficult times that we have the opportunity to experience the Lord's presence in a deeper way. When we cling to Him, He will reveal the good things that are right in front of us. God often allows hard things to happen in our lives in order to bless us in some way. If we are willing to allow for that possibility in everything that happens, it keeps us from being devastated by people and situations that are ultimately going to be used for God's glory. When we ask Him to show us the good in our difficult situations, He will.

7. *Pray that all your expectations will be in God alone.* Disappointment and suffering are inevitable because life can never consistently meet our expectations. Things certainly don't always turn out the way we want them to. But when we put our expectations in the Lord and acknowledge that our help comes from Him, it takes the pressure off others to meet our needs. We make a mistake by expecting too much from people, life, and ourselves when our expectations should be in God. It pleases Him when we have faith enough in the midst of our disappointment to put our hope and expectations in Him. Don't run into the arms of bitterness or unforgiveness. Run to your Father's arms instead so He can hold and sustain you.

8. *Pray that you will forgive others.* Often our greatest times of hurt, trial, difficulty, or disappointment occur when someone fails us—or we feel they have. People can hurt us deeply. But our fulfillment and happiness don't depend on other people, they depend on God. Of course we rely on other people for certain things and it's painful when they let us down. But the ultimate success or joy of our life doesn't depend on them. We have to forgive and release them and not continue to suffer

over what others do or don't do to us. Ultimately our reward is in God's hands. If we surrender our disappointment to God and say, "Be my light and lead me through this, Lord," then His work will be accomplished faster. But if we wallow in the darkness of bitterness, casting blame toward God and other people, we end up suffering more.

9. *Pray that God will help you forgive yourself.* It's devastating when we believe we have failed in some way or are responsible for the bad thing that has happened, perhaps due to our own carelessness or in spite of our best efforts. Or we think we have failed when we really haven't at all and we torture ourselves, allowing our regret and condemnation to pound our souls like a giant sledgehammer. It's a weight we can't carry and were never meant to. Even when we have to bear the consequences for the wrong choices we've made, God is still there to bring good out of it. Even in our greatest depth of failure, God redeems everything when we reach humbly to Him. While it is good to examine our motives, thoughts, and actions, it's counterproductive to beat ourselves up with a constant battering of: "If only I hadn't . . ." "If I just would have . . ." "Why didn't I . . ." for everything that goes wrong.

10. *Pray that you will not get discouraged.* Discouragement can descend on you like a flood. You think you are standing strong and all of a sudden, in a weary moment, you get washed away by discouragement that threatens to drown you. Even though it may seem like forever as you wait for your difficult time to end, and you feel like you don't have the strength to withstand anything any longer, tell yourself that you can do all things through Christ who strengthens you (Philippians 4:13). Declare that you will "rest in the LORD, and wait patiently for Him" (Psalm 37:7). Keep in mind that God has been known to do a quick work for which He has been preparing a long time. It could be today.

STRENGTH TO GO ON

Regardless of your present situation, know that God has an abundance of blessings for you. He is working powerfully in your life right where you are, so don't stop praying. Close your eyes, call His name, and sense His presence. He wants you to trust that when you are afraid, you can turn to Him and find His peace. When you are weary, you will find His strength. When you are empty, you will find His fullness. When you are sad, you will find His joy. And when you are in the middle of a raging storm, you will find His shelter and provision. Don't let yourself be blinded by circumstances, afraid of what's happening, easily discouraged, drawn toward bitterness, or quick to complain. Instead, look for God in the midst of your circumstances.

When you're disappointed, ask God to help you discern His truth about what you are experiencing. Instead of being consumed with the pain of it, look for revelation in the situation. Maintain a humble, submitted, faith-filled, expectant heart and you will see God's goodness manifest in the midst of all that's happening. He will use this experience to bring you closer to Him, and your greatest treasure will be a deep sense of His presence. He will make things right and He is the only one who can.

Remember that no matter how dark your situation may become, He is the light of your life and His light can never be put out. No matter what dark clouds settle on you, He will lift you above the storm and into the comfort of His presence. Only God can take whatever loss you experience and fill that empty place with good. Only God can take the burden of your grief and pain and dry your tears. Invite Him to do that. And every time you rise above the difficulties in your life and find the goodness, clarity, peace, and light of the Lord there, your faith will increase. God will meet you in the midst of your pain and not only perfect you, but also increase your compassion for the sufferings of others. As you continue to live in the presence of the Lord, His glory will be revealed in you.

If God was able to get me through those long eighteen months of pain and struggle, He can also get you through whatever difficulties you are going through. He is there for you. Don't miss Him in the midst of your suffering. Draw close to Him and let Him heal and purify you and bring you into new knowledge of Him.

A PRAYER FOR HELP IN DIFFICULT TIMES

Lord, I give thanks to You in all things because I know that You reign in the midst of them. I know that when I pass through the waters, You will be with me and the river will not flow over me. When I walk through the fire, I will not be burned. Nor will the flame touch me (Isaiah 43:1–2). That's because You are a good God and have sent Your Holy Spirit to be my Comforter and Helper in the midst of difficult times.

Lord, I wait for You today. I put my hope in Your Word and ask that You would fill me afresh with Your Holy Spirit and wash away all anxiety or doubt. Shine Your light into any dark corner of my soul that needs to be exposed. I don't want my impatience or lack of trust to stand in the way of all You desire to do in my life at this time. I realize that no matter how difficult life gets, as long as I cling to You I am moving forward on the path you have for me. Help me to wait on You and not grow impatient with my circumstances simply because my timetable does not coincide with Yours. Help me to understand Your ways and not give in to discouragement. Strengthen my faith to depend on Your perfect timing for my life. Help me to rest in You and be content with where I am right now. At the same time, I ask you to heal, restore, redeem, transform, and bring new life to my situation. Teach me what I need to learn and help me get beyond this time successfully so I can rise above the storm to Your place of perfect peace. Amen.

ABOUT THE AUTHOR

Stormie Omartian is the best-selling author of *The Power of a Praying Woman, The Power of a Praying Wife, The Power of a Praying Husband,* and *The Power of a Praying Parent.* She is an accomplished songwriter and has toured throughout the nation as a speaker for Aspiring Women conferences. Stormie and her husband, Grammy-winning record producer Michael Omartian, have been married twenty-nine years and have three grown children.

VERSES THAT INSPIRE

> [God] answered their prayers, because they trusted in him. (1 Chronicles 5:20)

> This is the confidence we have in approaching God: that if we ask anything according to his will, he hears us. (1 John 5:14)

For the eyes of the Lord are on the righteous and his ears are attentive to their prayer. (1 Peter 3:12)

Be joyful always; pray continually, give thanks in all circumstances, for this is God's will for you in Christ Jesus. (1 Thessalonians 5:16–18)

Living beyond Life's Circumstances

JONI EARECKSON TADA

Come near to God and he will come near to you.

—JAMES 4:8

When I was injured in a diving accident many years ago, I spent a lot of time talking to counselors and therapists. I had just been paralyzed from the neck down and I was asked a variety of basic questions about my psyche and self-esteem. But I had some big-issue questions I wanted to ask them: "How am I going to manage through life like this? Will I ever *not* be depressed? What about my future?" Sad to say, they didn't offer me any answers. As a Christian, however, I knew (in a vague sort of way) that the Bible probably had some answers to my problems. When I was in the hospital, I had plenty of time to search the Scriptures since I was placed on a "Stryker frame" for an entire year. A Stryker frame turned me into a long, flat canvas sandwich. I would lay faceup for a couple of hours and then the nurses would strap another piece of canvas on top of me, flip me over, and I would then lie facedown. While I was in this "down" position, I used a mouth stick in my teeth and laboriously turned the pages of my Bible, searching for answers.

But I became irritated with the Bible. Everything I read seemed so out of touch with my reality. I kept coming across phrases like "we rejoice in our sufferings." As a Reformed Episcopalian, I tried to recall what I knew from the *Book of Common Prayer*, a verse or two, or a hymn. But that didn't help much either.

After a year I was transferred off the Stryker frame and my depression sank deeper as the reality of my situation began to sink in. The nurses put me in a ward with five other girls, and there were many nights when I would want so desperately to cry, but I didn't. You see, if I cried my tears would well up in my eyes and sting. At night there was nobody to help me blow my nose, and since I didn't want to be messy, I wouldn't let myself cry—so I became a bit of a stoic back then. Of course, people often ask me, when did the change come? Where was the turning point? What was the passage that turned your life around?

During my endless months in the hospital, I was so grateful for my Christian friends who would come and visit. They carried their Bibles, but they also brought along their guitars, their pizza, and their Simon & Garfunkel albums. And I'd pester them with my questions. It was my varsity hockey buddy, Jackie—who was just another kid like me, but she loved Jesus—who helped me overcome my depression. I had asked her, "Why me? How am I going to manage this?" It's a funny thing about the question "why?" It's never dry, abstract, or theoretical. It's not like walking up to a chalk-board and scratching out a quick solution. Suffering is never cool, detached, or unemotional. It can't be answered in a neat and tidy fashion. When we hurt, we ask "why?" with intense emotion. We're angry! I was so grateful for my friends, especially Jackie, who seemed, in a very naive, seventeen-year-old kind of way, to be able to absorb my anger as well as my questions.

One night when my roommates were asleep and I was struggling with one of those "mad midnight" moments at 2 A.M., I was so tired of being a stoic. Suddenly, I turned my head and saw coming through the doorway of my ward a figure crawling on hands and knees. In the shadows, I couldn't tell who it was, but the person crept closer, sneaking past my roommates in the dark until her hands reached up to the guardrail of my hospital bed and she peered up at me.

"Jackie!" I exclaimed. "Jackie, if they catch you, they're going to kick you out of here!"

"Shh," she whispered. I later learned that after visiting hours, she hid in the visitors' lounge behind a sofa so that when the nurses went on break, she could crawl to my bedside. She stood up and put her hands on the guardrail and lowered it. And then, as seventeen-year-old kids will do, especially girlfriends who have enjoyed one another's company at many a pajama party, she crept into bed with me, snuggled up close, put her head on my pillow, and didn't say a word.

But softly in the shadows so as to not awake my roommates, she began to sing. "Man of sorrows, what a name for the Son of God who came, ruined sinners to reclaim, hallelujah, what a Savior." And then, she took my hand in hers, intertwined our fingers (she knew my paralysis was so bad that I could not feel her hand), and she held up my hand so that I could see. Then she softly began to sing that hymn again. "Man of sorrows, what a name for the Son of God who came, ruined sinners to reclaim, hallelujah, what a Savior."

I know God has the answers. Thirty-five years of paralysis has been like a classroom for me as I've discovered the richness and depth and wonder and sweet satisfaction of all that the Word of God contains for people who are suffering. God has His reasons—a refined faith, a stronger character, and a purified heart are just a few answers to the question "Why?" But when you're hurting, and your heart is being squeezed like a sponge, or you're feeling numb and you don't know if your emotions are upside down or right side up, a list of sixteen biblical reasons that all of this is happening can sting like salt in a wound. The bleeding doesn't simply stop when someone ticks off answers, although they may be good and right and true. When you're grieving over the loss of your body or other personal struggles, answers don't often reach the hurt that's down in your gut and heart. When a person is suffering like I was when I was first injured, you're like a child who's been hurt and you turn to your big, strong father and say, "Daddy, why?" Now, I don't think it's very daddy-like for the father to look down at his child and say with cold detachment, "Well, child, I'm so glad you asked that question. You see, my plan for you in all of this is 'such and so'." No, a child who's hurt wants her daddy to reach down and pick her up and press her against his chest and say, "There, there, honey, everything's going to be okay. Daddy's here."

That's our heartfelt plea, isn't it? We want assurance. Better yet, we want fatherly assurance that there is an order to our painful reality that somehow transcends our problems. We want assurance that our world is not splitting apart at the seams. We want assurance that our world is orderly and stable and somehow safe. We want God to be at the center of things, to be in control. He must be at the center of our suffering and He must be good. He must be our "daddy"—warm, kind, and compassionate. This is our cry when we ask "why?" The problem of suffering is not about something; it's about someone. And so it follows that the answer is not something, but someone. And God, like any good daddy, doesn't give answers as much as He gives Himself.

When this began to sink in, at the end of two years in the hospital, there were nights when I stopped being stoic and instead visualized Jesus coming to visit me. I didn't actually see Him, but I imagined Him breaking the rules just like Jackie had, sneaking into

> *God, like any good daddy, doesn't give answers as much as He gives Himself.*

my six-bed ward. And He would walk over to my bed, put down the guardrail, and sit on the edge of my mattress. With one hand, He would gently brush back my hair, and with the other He would show me the scars where nails had pierced Him. And He'd say to me, "Joni, if I loved you enough to die for you, then can't you trust Me with the answers?" God, like a good daddy, offers Himself to us. In Psalm 18, He becomes the high fortress to a person like me who is struggling for answers and wanting to be rescued. In Psalm 2, He becomes the Father to the orphan. In Isaiah 62, He becomes the

Bridegroom to the widow. In Isaiah 54, He is the Husband to the single woman who's afraid she'll never marry. And in Exodus 15, He's the Healer to the sick. In Isaiah 9, He is a wonderful Counselor to the manic-depressive. In John 4, He explains that He is living water to those who are thirsty, and in John 6, He is the gate to heaven for those who are hungry for more than this world can offer.

How or why God created suffering is not the question. The point is, He's the answer and we need Him. And that's what Jackie reminded me the night she crawled into my hospital room. "Man of sorrows." She didn't say anything else but that. And so I began to understand an extremely important truth: God is good. And in subsequent years, as I continued to flip through the Bible with my mouth stick, I realized more and more, God is good. He is supremely good in the midst of suffering, yes, because He *gives* us answers, but more so because He *is* the answer. He doesn't offer us lots of words; He is the Word. And if you're the one who's at the center of the universe, if you're like Acts 17:28 and everything moves and breathes and has its being in you, you can do no more than give yourself. If you've given yourself, you've given everything.

I learned early on in this wheelchair that God owed me no explanations. He did enough explaining on the cross. He didn't provide me with the words I was looking for at the beginning of my paralysis. Instead, He is the Word. The Word made flesh, hands nearly ripped off, nailed to a cross, vomit, spit, smeared, dried blood, hammering hatred, flies buzzing. These aren't merely facts about the love of the Lord Jesus. As a saint once said, "This is love poured out like wine as strong as fire." And for one who suffers, I'm so glad Jesus endured a messy death on the cross. I'm so grateful that our God isn't a medicating mystic of a guru who sits on some mountaintop, twiddling his thumbs, but is our Savior who suffered a messy, bloody death that was excruciatingly painful at the hands of vindictive and mean-spirited men.

God allows suffering so that nothing stands between Him and me. You see, when we suffer, we're much more apt to fall to our knees, and when we do, our hearts are open to the Lord. And then nothing will separate us from the love of Christ—not trouble, hardship, danger, or the sword. "For I am convinced that neither death nor life, neither angels nor demons, neither the present nor the future, nor any powers . . . will be able to separate us from the love of God that is in Christ Jesus, our Lord" (Romans 8:38). Naturally we doubt the goodness of God when we experience divorce or depression or read the headlines about tens of thousands killed in an earthquake in Turkey. And we'll continue to doubt Him unless we begin to see the goodness of God that is in Jesus. We've got to look at Jesus. God has a different perspective than you and I when it comes to hardships, headaches, broken necks, and broken homes. Whether it's violence, war, divorce, or clinical depression, God permits, allows, ordains, or decrees it, whichever verb you choose. Satan doesn't run the world's agenda; God does. And if He didn't, He'd be doing nothing but reacting to devilish schemes and we all know that is not the God of the Bible.

Why does God have this world rigged for frustration, wired for pain, and devastated by disappointment? After thirty-five years of paralysis, I think I can finally answer that question confidently. Tomorrow morning when I wake up, I will hear my girlfriend running the water in the bathroom in our hotel room, then she'll dial room service for coffee. My eyes won't quite be open yet, but I will whisper, "God, I don't think I can take another day of this. Lord, for me to live is

You, but I'll tell you what, to die would be gain. I'm so tired. I'm so weary of this pain in the back of my neck and my shoulder. Isn't it enough that I'm paralyzed? I mean, haven't I filled my life's quota for trials? Why do I have to put up with this pain? And God, I can't even face my friend with a smile this morning. I need You, I need You desperately. I require You. I am urgently asking You for help. Help me, Lord Jesus. I don't have a smile for my friend or for anybody this morning, so please let me borrow Your smile. I need You."

I think it was M. Scott Peck who said in one of his books, "Life is supposed to be difficult." My favorite statement in his book echoed the words of Jesus: "In this world you will have trouble" (John 16:33). And I guess this is why I love 2 Corinthians 4:7–10, which says, in essence, "Though we are handicapped on all sides, we're not crushed. Though we're perplexed, we're not in despair. Though we are persecuted, we're not abandoned. Though we are knocked down, we are not knocked out."

Everyday life is supposed to be difficult. Every day we're supposed to experience something of the death of the Lord

Jesus Christ so that in turn, we might experience power and the life of Jesus in these bodies of ours.

And then, lo and behold, when my girlfriend comes to my bedside with a cup of coffee and pulls down my covers, I turn my head to her and I suddenly have a smile. But it didn't come from me. It came straight from heaven.

Abraham Lincoln once said, "It is this weakness that keeps driving us, driving us to God by the overwhelming conviction that we've got nowhere else to go. There is no help but Him. There is no hope but Him." I asked my physical therapist if there was some way to ease the pain in my neck and shoulders. I was so hoping there might be some kind of medication or treatment. But my only hope is in Jesus. Isn't it funny how He's got it rigged? We have to go to Him for strength and help, hope and perspective, even the ability to smile. In fact, all of us have a double blessing. Philippians 3:20–21 says, "We eagerly await a Savior from [heaven], the Lord Jesus Christ, who . . . will transform our lowly bodies so that they will be like his glorious body." No wonder Romans tells us to be joyful in hope. If we really understood what we will one day experience in heaven, we would be much more joyful. Even in our sorrow, we'd be rejoicing. We have nothing, yet we have everything in our future hope. One day, I will have a new body. And Revelation 7:17 says that God personally will wipe away our tears. Isn't that great? God will personally wipe away my tears. And isn't it ironic that when I finally regain use of my hands in order to dry my own eyes, I won't have any tears to wipe away?

Larry Crabb once said something to this effect: "The earth was never meant to keep its promises." The world crushes our illusions for a reason—we have no business becoming comfortable down here on an earth that is destined to decay. Suffering squeezes our shoes so that earth's shoes don't fit, which forces us to put our other foot in heaven. So one day, when I'm in my brand-new, splendorous body, I will stand up on resurrected legs and raise my hands up high, spread my fingers, and shout to everybody in the entire universe, "Worthy is the Lamb, who was slain, to receive power and wealth and wisdom and strength and honor and glory and praise" (Revelation 5:12). I am but a little bud down here on earth, but one day I will blossom.

And with this new glorified body will come a new glorified heart. People often think I'm most excited about a new body, but I can't wait for a new heart. No more half-hearted, ho-hum praise for the Lord. No more distractions. No more small-minded meanspiritedness. No more petty vindictiveness. No more confession of sin, even though I dearly love the confession in the *Book of Common Prayer* that says, "Almighty and resourceful Father, we like sheep have erred and strayed. We have gone our own way. We have followed too much the devises and desires of our own hearts. We have offended against Thy holy laws. We have left undone those things that we ought to have done and we have done those things that we ought not have done."

So when I get to heaven in my new resurrected body, this is what I hope to do. It may be theologically incorrect, but I hope I can take my old wheelchair with me. Not my streamlined travel model, but my old Sherman tank that I use in Southern California—my old clunky, dusty wheelchair. That's what I want beside me when I'm standing before Jesus, because then I'll be able to say, "Lord Jesus, do You see this thing? Well, before You send it to hell, there's something I want to tell You. I was in this thing for more than three decades and You were right, in this world I did have trouble. But the more troublesome life was in that wheelchair, the more I leaned on You. And the more I leaned on You, Lord, the stronger I discovered You to be. The affliction was light and momentary compared to the privilege it was to share in the fellowship of Your sufferings. You died for sin, I died to sin, and that's how I became like You in Your death. And if I had not been paralyzed, I don't think I would have cared about such stuff. But Lord, in the process of sharing in Your suffering, I became much closer to You. I felt Your strength. I was able to reveal to others Your smile, and miraculously, my heart beat in rhythm to Yours."

People have asked me, "If you could, would you be healed?" I always tell them, "Sure, but not if it jeopardized my intimacy with God in this place of pain." Remember those Bible verses I mentioned earlier that were once so irritating and out of touch with reality? Verses like "consider your afflictions light and momentary"? That kind of mind-set is only possible when we contrast it to heaven. Heaven is the bottom line for Christians. And don't ever think of it as some psychological crutch that shouldn't be mentioned. Heaven is definitely reality! Earth is but the title page of our lives. The real story is yet to unfold and we should reinforce ourselves with the heart-pumping hope of heaven.

Afflictions, in a strange way, are nothing more than momentary discomforts when they point people to Jesus. Do you struggle with hurts? Do you feel rejected? Do you feel forsaken by your husband? Jesus was the most God-forsaken man who ever lived. And do you know why? So He could say to those in need, "I will never leave you. I will never forsake you." Are you lonely, forgotten by your friends? Jesus Himself couldn't even make His three best friends spend one hour with Him in prayer at the most critical time of His life (Mark 14:37). If you feel like the world has passed you by, it did the same thing to Jesus first. Does God descend into your hell? Yes, He does. Dr. Peter Kreeft said, "You can endure almost anything, even sitting slumped in a hospital bed, dying of cancer—you can endure almost anything if you know God is sitting next to you."

Unending Sorrow

Not long ago I celebrated my high school reunion. I was excited about showing off my husband, Ken. We'd been married seventeen years and living in Southern California. It was going to be so much fun to hop on a plane and fly east to show all my high school friends my husband and find out what they had been doing with their lives. I called the chairman of the reunion committee and said, "Boy, is this going to be fun. I'm so looking forward to seeing Tommy and Linda Snuff. And I'm really excited about seeing my friend Jackie. My good old hockey buddy." But there was a silence on the other end of the phone.

"Oh, Joni," my friend said. "Didn't you hear? Well, no, I guess you couldn't have, because it happened last night. It was on the evening news."

"No, what happened?" I asked. I knew Jackie had experienced some tough times in recent years. Her husband had left her with two children. One of them had really been struggling with a bout of depression. He made a profession of faith and then stepped back from it and became involved with the wrong crowd.

"Well, Jackie's son set himself on fire in his father's house last night and burned down the entire place, including himself. He left a suicide note in the mailbox. I don't think Jackie will be coming to the reunion, Joni." I hung up and immediately tried to telephone my old friend, but I couldn't get through. So I did the next best thing: I wrote my friend a letter:

Dear Jackie,

Ken and I are planning to be in Baltimore and I'm hoping we can see each other then. If so, I would want to hold your hand as you once held mine in the hospital. And I would sing softly to you as you once sang to me "Man of Sorrows." I don't know what else to say but that. May the Man of Sorrows be your comfort. And just like in the hospital, I hope you, too, would feel what I once felt and I still remember to this day: a strange sense of peace over me. Not answers, but peace. Do you remember that night thirty years ago? I have never forgotten it.

Ken and I did make it to the reunion, and we did share a quiet dinner with Jackie just before the reunion. We didn't talk about answers. The pain was still too fresh. But she said this to me: "Whenever I lose my balance," she said as she clasped the gold cross that hung around her neck, "I remember this: When you're hurting, when your heart aches with pain, when you've just become a quadriplegic or your husband leaves you or your son commits suicide, trying to find the answers is pointless. They are there and they will come in time. But there is a place, probably the most important place in a person's recovery, when he is pressed up against the bloody cross, which smells of urine and sweat and the stench of Christ's death. And as Thomas Bentley said, 'The only answer that satisfies is to think on that greater affliction, Christ on the cross.' One day He will give us the key that will unlock everything and it will help us make sense of it all. Until then, leaning on the Man of Sorrows is enough."

ABOUT THE AUTHOR

Joni Eareckson Tada is the founder and president of Joni and Friends. She has authored more than twenty books, serves as a presidential appointee to the National Council on Disability, and is a columnist for *Moody* magazine. Her radio program reaches millions of listeners on over seven hundred stations throughout the United States, although her ministry itself is worldwide. Joni has been married to Ken Tada since 1982.

VERSES THAT INSPIRE

On my bed I remember you;
    I think of you through the watches of the night.
Because you are my help,
    I sing in the shadow of your wings.
My soul clings to you;
    Your right hand upholds me.
(Psalm 63:6–8)

But if we hope for what we do not yet have, we wait for it patiently. (Romans 8:25)

You will weep no more. How gracious he will be when you cry for help! As soon as he hears, he will answer you. (Isaiah 30:19)

Now to him who is able to do immeasurably more than all we ask or imagine, according to his power that is at work within us, to him be glory in the church and in Christ Jesus throughout all generations, for ever and ever! Amen.
(Ephesians 3:20–21)

Handling Conflict

LESLIE VERNICK

Blessed are the peacemakers,
for they will be called sons of God.

—MATTHEW 5:9

When I was a little girl, one of the first nursery rhymes I ever learned was "Sugar and spice and everything nice, that's what little girls are made of." Boys, however, are made out of "snakes and snails and puppy dog tails," such nasty stuff. Unfortunately, the legacy of all sweetness has followed us into womanhood. We don't have conflicts, do we? Certainly not if we are *Christian* women.

As I pondered this, I thought back to my own childhood and the things I learned as a little girl about handling disagreement. My heroines from my favorite bedtime stories taught me a lot.

First there was Snow White, who lived in a castle with her father, though he wasn't around much, and her wicked stepmother who despised Snow White because she was so beautiful. Snow White, always innocent, was oblivious to her stepmother's hatred and seemed genuinely surprised when the hunter explained that her stepmother wanted her dead. But Snow White didn't grapple with conflict. She also didn't talk to anybody about it; she simply decided to run away and ended up living with the Seven Dwarfs. When Snow White's stepmother eventually found her and gave her a poison apple, she needed a handsome prince to rescue her.

My second childhood heroine was Cinderella. Poor, sweet, innocent Cinderella lived with her stepmother and two ugly stepsisters. She was in perpetual conflict with all three of them—but she never spoke up. She never mentioned their mistreatment of her to anyone. But Cinderella did have a fairy godmother to help her. And she was rescued by a handsome prince.

My third heroine was Sleeping Beauty. Similar dynamics, but by now you're getting the picture. Women from my era grew up believing that girls grew up to become either beautiful, sweet, and helpless women or ugly, mean, and wicked ones. Those were the two options. We had few female role models who were strong and kind, sweet and firm. They were either passive or aggressive.

Understandably, some of us grew up perceiving ourselves as the Cinderella type. And as Christian women we may feel even more uncomfortable around conflict than our non-Christian contemporaries because we also embrace the command to love others as Christ loved us. But we struggle with how to honor that command while also living out the biblical mandates to speak the truth in love, admonish the unruly, confront sin, and be salt and light to the earth.

In fact, as Christians we can be faced with a downright dilemma at times: Should we forbear and forgive, or speak up and confront? What do you do when you face conflict in your workplace, church, or home? Do you withdraw? Are you the passive type, remaining silent? Or maybe you're more aggressive; you speak your mind without any thought or prayer beforehand.

CONFLICT AND ITS CAUSES

Conflict stems from opposing viewpoints between one or more people. Sometimes it causes a disagreement, but at other times it invites valuable discussion. Typically, however, conflict erupts when we disagree with someone's thoughts, feelings, or values, and a discussion ensues in which each person argues his or her perspective. In essence, we are trying to defend our position and hopefully convince the other person to see it our way. Now, there are lots of reasons that conflicts erupt, but let's consider three of them.

1. *Conflict can arise when we disapprove of someone.* In Numbers 12, Miriam disapproves of Moses' decision to marry a Cushite woman. As a result, she stirs up discord in the camp and says things like, "Has the Lord indeed only spoken through Moses? He's spoken through us as well"

(Numbers 12:2). Maybe a similar situation has happened to you. Someone has disapproved of you or your actions and they've talked about you behind your back. They are purposely creating conflict. Or maybe you've disapproved of someone or what they've done. Are you dealing directly with them or are you talking with others more along the lines of gossip? Are your actions stirring up conflict at work or church?

2. *Conflict can occur because of jealousy.* 1 Samuel 29 contains the story of King Saul and David. At first they enjoyed a good relationship. David even played the harp for King Saul. But when David killed Goliath, David's popularity soared, which made Saul jealous. Eventually conflict arose between them. It wasn't really due to discord in their relationship, but it was rather an issue of Saul's own heart. He was jealous of David.

3. *Conflict can result from selfishness.* James 4:1–2 says, "What causes fights and quarrels among you? Don't they come from your desires that battle within you? You want something but don't get it. You kill and covet, but you cannot have what you want." Sometimes we're jealous of one

another. Sometimes we're just plain selfish. We argue because we're not getting what we want.

But let's clarify something—wanting something or asking for something is *not* being selfish. Selfishness occurs when we demand things without considering the other person's feelings or desires. All we care about is getting our own way. And when we're in that mindset, conflict is bound to happen because other people are not always willing to bow to our demands.

4. *Conflicts can erupt when someone causes you pain or suffering.* The Bible refers to that as being "sinned against." Sometimes, of course, this can happen in small ways. Perhaps my husband forgets to stop at the grocery store in spite of being reminded three times. In these instances, God asks us to be forbearing because love should cover a multitude of sins. In other situations, however, when someone repeats an offense or causes a great deal of pain, we must not keep silent. Peace at any cost cannot and should not always be maintained. Something has damaged the relationship. To keep silent is not what God intended when He called us to be peacemakers. Sometimes we must speak up and risk a conflict in order

to bring about a resolution to the relationship, or at least bring to someone's attention the need for responsibility and repentance.

5. *Conflicts occur because people simply are different.* We don't always think alike. We must be willing to listen to another person's point of view and consider their perspective, or conflict will certainly occur.

Here's how one woman from the Bible handled conflict. Queen Esther certainly found herself in the midst of turmoil, but rather than keeping silent, she risked her relationship with the king to bring peace to a very difficult situation. It all began when Haman, an official of the king, was promoted and given authority over all the other servants. He required everyone to honor him by bowing to him. A lone Jew named Mordecai refused to bow down to Haman, because he believed God instructed him to bow down to the only One worthy of this action, who was God. And so a conflict arose between Haman and Mordecai. Haman became so enraged by Mordecai's convictions that he tricked the king into signing a law that all Jews would be killed on a certain date.

Fortunately, Mordecai was Esther's uncle. "Esther," he

said, "you've got to do something. You've got to talk to the king about this law or all of us will be killed" (Esther 4:8, 12–14, my paraphrase). Suddenly our docile queen is thrown into a conflict she had nothing to do with. How would you handle such a situation?

Let's consider a modern-day scenario. Your boss asks you to do something that compromises your convictions just a bit. What would you do? Would you be like Mordecai and refuse? Would you stand up for what you believe or would you just go along with it to keep peace? Would you speak up even if it cost you your job?

You're probably just as scared as Esther. She didn't know what to do, but she knew she couldn't be passive. She knew she had to do something. Naturally it was tempting to preserve her own safety and position as the queen and keep silent. But that would have been wrong. She also wasn't aggressive. She could have marched right into the king's throne room and said, "I can't believe you signed such a stupid law!" However, queens were only allowed to enter the king's throne room if they were invited. For this reason, Esther feared for her life. These days, we're not so much afraid to approach people because of physical harm, but because we're afraid they'll reject us or laugh at us or think our perspective is stupid or wrong. Or maybe we could lose our job or be blacklisted, hindering future promotions. And so we keep quiet, saying nothing. In these instances, what are we to do? Should we be passive or aggressive? Fortunately, God provides a third way.

Jesus tells us, "Blessed are the peacemakers, for they will be called sons of God" (Matthew 5:9). God doesn't want us to remain still. Too many Christian women see passivity as a fruit of the Spirit. We refer to it as "submission" or as a "quiet and gentle spirit." But sometimes we don't speak up when we should. Such situations involving abuse or injustice, domestic violence, or things that hurt others and our relationships need to be addressed.

A client of mine discovered that her husband was having an affair with one of his colleagues, but she never confronted him. She decided she was going to wait it out, to forbear. Sometimes women are applauded for their great patience. But my client's patience did not come from the Holy Spirit. Her do-nothing posture came out of fear—not faith. Fear of what her husband would say, fear of conflict, fear of dissolution of the relationship. But fear is not a fruit of the Spirit.

Remember this: Jesus doesn't call us to be peace*keepers;* He calls us to be peace*makers.*

BEING A PEACEMAKER

Let's identify what a peacemaker is and does, in order to understand what God would want us to do to bring about peace. Psalm 34:14 says, "Turn

True peacemaking only happens when we're empowered by God.

from evil and do good; seek peace and pursue it." Hebrews 12:14 says, "Live in peace with all men." And Romans 12:18 says, "If it is possible, as far as it depends on you, live at peace with everyone." So a peacemaker pursues peace. To pursue is a definite action; it is not passive. It's something we must *do.* Withdrawing from conflict might give you an illusion of peace, but it's not real peace. *Shalom* is a Hebrew word that means peace, but it implies a willingness to risk conflict in order to bring about a genuine peace in a relationship. Peacemaking does not come naturally to humans. True peace-making only happens when we're empowered by God. A biblical peacemaker is not an easygoing, peace-at-any-price person who does whatever is necessary in order to avoid confrontation. We all know people like this. They often run in second gear. They're never too passionate about anything, because they never let anything bother them—they are peace-keepers.

In our story of Queen Esther, Mordecai certainly could have acquiesced to Haman's demand and bowed down to him. No big deal, right? God would have known he wasn't *really* compromising his convictions when he bowed to Haman. Wrong. Mordecai could have attempted a semblance of peace, but it would not have been true peace because God's law and His holiness would have been compromised. Mordecai was willing to stand up for what he believed, knowing that it would bring him into conflict with Haman.

The Bible is full of examples of those who were willing to enter into conflict in order to deal with problems and promote true peace. Paul confronted Peter, when Peter showed favoritism to the circumcised Jews (Galatians 2:11–13). John the Baptist confronted Herod about his adulterous affair (Matthew 14:3–5). Nathan spoke to David about his affair with Bathsheba and the murder of her husband (2 Samuel 12:1–7). Aquila and Priscilla approached Apollos when they believed he was teaching incorrect doctrine because they wanted to be sure he understood accurately (Acts 18:24–28). And Jesus confronted the Pharisees, not because He wanted to tell them they were wrong, but because He wanted them to know the truth. Only then would they possess genuine peace (Matthew 23:23–35).

A biblical peacemaker doesn't operate from her own agenda. In fact, she doesn't even come by those qualities naturally; they are gifts of the Spirit. A genuine peacemaker empties herself of her own self-consciousness, her own selfish motives, her own self-interest. A peacemaker is interested in giving glory to God or putting the interest of the other person first or restoring a relationship. If you're more concerned with your own needs and interests, you cannot be a genuine peacemaker.

ACHIEVING THE PEACEMAKER'S GOALS

So far we've considered both the mindset and the goals of a peacemaker. Now let's look at examples from Scripture to see how these goals are achieved.

1. *Learn to listen and see the other's viewpoint.* James tells us to be slow to speak but quick to listen (James 1:19). But oftentimes we don't listen very well, do we? Even with our friends, we're sometimes more interested in what we want to say than in listening to their concerns. If you want to be a genuine peacemaker, you must learn to listen and to see things from another person's point of view.

When I'm involved in counseling couples, they often will argue right in front of me. One couple I worked with disagreed often but they never resolved their differences because they never respectfully listened to one another. They constantly interrupted each other. Finally I stopped them and asked the wife to listen quietly while her husband shared his point of view. She folded her arms, rolled her eyes, and said, "Okay, talk," but her heart wasn't receptive and he knew it. We need to ask God for a heart and mind that are willing to listen to the other person's concerns and feelings and not only be concerned with our own.

While listening, don't attack the other person's perspective or feelings. If you do, he or she will be a lot less willing to expose him- or herself to critical scrutiny. Try really hard to see things from his or her perspective. There is not always a right and wrong way in every situation. Be willing to consider opinions or perspectives you did not originally endorse. Be flexible. As Philippians 2:3–4 says, "Do nothing from selfishness or empty conceit. But with humility of mind let each of you regard one another as more important than himself. Do not merely look out for your own personal interests, but also for the interests of others" (NASB). This verse doesn't say don't look out for your own interests; it says, don't look out for your own interests *alone*, but also consider the interests of others. If we want to be peacemakers, we need to care about the interests, concerns, thoughts, feelings, and perspectives of others.

2. *Speak the truth, but in a loving manner.* Look at Ephesians 4 to see how to become a skilled peacemaker. Conflicts can make us feel angry, but the Bible tells us not to sin in our anger. If we need to speak up, we need to do it with a loving

attitude. Consider 1 Corinthians 13, which says that if we speak with the tongues of angels but do not have love in our heart, we are going to be like a gong, a clanging symbol. It's difficult for the other person to hear the truth if it's said in anger or disrespect. The other person will become defensive, rather than receptive. On the other hand, Proverbs 27:5–6 says, "Better is open rebuke than love that is concealed. Faithful are the wounds of a friend, but deceitful are the kisses of an enemy." Women need to resist the temptation to shut down their feelings and perspectives simply to preserve peace. Sometimes it's crucial that we speak up.

Debbie was one of my clients, and she was very passive. A people-pleaser by nature, she never knew how to say no. Her friend Lorraine decided that since Debbie didn't work outside the home and Lorraine did, she would ask Debbie to do her laundry because she was desperately behind. Being a kindhearted person, Debbie told Lorraine she'd be glad to help her. So Lorraine brought over her laundry and Debbie washed it, folded it, put it back in the basket, and returned it to Lorraine. Next week, guess what? Lorraine dropped her laundry off and Debbie did it again. Week after week,

Lorraine brought her dirty laundry and Debbie did it, because she didn't know how to say no. Is that like you? Are you initially willing to help but then become resentful?

Instead of telling Lorraine she couldn't do her laundry anymore, Debbie began to lock her screen door so Lorraine had no place to leave the laundry. Debbie was afraid to speak up because she knew it would cause a conflict between them. But by not speaking up, the relationship was definitely deteriorating because Sandy resented her friend's taking advantage of her. She finally mustered up all of her courage and said, "Lorraine, I was happy to do your laundry the first week, even the second week. But I really don't want to do your wash all the time. You're going to have to find someone else to do it or do it yourself." At first Lorraine became defensive and angry. But she eventually realized her friendship with Debbie was more important than her laundry. Debbie also learned an important lesson: She must learn to handle conflict in order to maintain her friendships. If she hadn't said anything to Lorraine, the relationship would have eventually ended. But Debbie learned to speak the truth in love to her friend—the true mark of a peacemaker.

Of course, we need to resist the urge to become recklessly honest. The longer Debbie allowed resentment to fester, the more tempted she was to blow up and insult Lorraine. But the Bible tells us that reckless words can pierce like a sword. Sometimes we become furious because we feel someone has taken advantage of us for too long or

> *We need to resist the urge to become recklessly honest.*

has hurt us deeply. When this happens, we explode. We give no thought to how to handle it in a loving, constructive manner—we just let it all out. I compare that to vomit. We feel much better once it's out of our system, but it really belongs in the toilet, not on another person. So be careful when you have a lot of strong feelings brewing inside. Make an effort to vent any destructive feelings in the least harmful way, such as putting them down in a journal or writing a letter you never intend to mail. If you can release your negativity before you approach the person you're angry with, you can eventually speak the truth in love and be constructive.

KNOWING WHEN TO CONFRONT

Not every little injustice that happens to you requires a confrontation. It's irritating to be in relationship with people who regularly tell us everything we do that bothers them. The Bible instructs us to be forbearing, to give people the benefit of the doubt. But there are other times and other situations that require us to speak out. So how do we know the difference?

There are three criteria that I use to evaluate whether I need to speak the truth in love or forbear and wait patiently.

1. *Is this something that is dishonoring God?* Is a relationship or a situation dishonoring their testimony or our Lord? Romans 2:19–21 says, "[You] are confident that you yourself are a guide to the blind, a light to those who are in darkness, a corrector of the foolish, a teacher of the immature, having in the Law the embodiment of knowledge and of the truth, you, therefore, who teach another, do you not teach yourself? You who preach that one should not steal, do you steal?" (NASB). And the passage goes on to say in verse 23 that through breaking the law, you dishonor God. The

apostle Paul pointed out that there are people who have a position of authority or leadership and yet something in their lives dishonors God.

Many years ago my husband worked with a friend of ours who was active in our church. He was a very fine man in many respects, but he had a problem—he used foul language when he became angry. Perhaps at home he could get away with it and apologize afterward and people would understand that he was still in a growing process. But at work he spoke to others about the joy of God and his leadership responsibilities in the church. He would hand out tracts and invite people to Sunday worship, but when he became angry with people, he'd curse them. Often my husband, Howard, would hear a recounting of the day's difficulties complete with the cursing tirade. Finally, after much thought and prayer, Howard decided he needed to talk to this friend who professed to love God but then cursed and dishonored Him with his language. Peace needed to be restored, and this man could not continue to dishonor God and have peace. I'm thankful to report that this friend was receptive to Howard's comments and through the help of other men who held him accountable, he really began to work on his language for the glory of God. So when God is being dishonored, we must speak up and speak the truth, but always in love.

2. *Are the other person's actions causing self-inflicted damage?* Many of us have at least one friend who is standing a bit too close to the edge of a cliff. Maybe you have a girlfriend who's toying with the idea of adultery. Perhaps she is on the verge of abusing her children, whether physically or emotionally. Sometimes we know a person who is drinking too much or taking substances she shouldn't and it's hurting her. And yet we never say anything. I can't tell you the number of women I've met over the years who've been hurt by domestic violence or adulterous situations and who have longed for someone from their church to come alongside their wayward husband and say, "What are you doing? You're not only hurting your spouse, you're hurting yourself. How can I help?"

Galatians 6:1 tells us that whenever someone is caught in a trespass, we are to restore that person in a spirit of gentleness. When we see someone doing something harmful to themselves or others, we must keep in mind that restoration is our goal and proceed gently. When an old building is slated for restoration, the foreman doesn't go in with a bull-dozer; he goes in with finely trained craftsmen who are going to restore that building to its original beauty. When you see someone struggling with a sinful situation in their life, don't level them like a bulldozer. Don't rip that person to shreds. (Unfortunately, this is often what happens.) Be gentle in order to bring about healing in their lives, to detangle them from the sin they've been caught in. All the while we must keep a check on our own lives lest we, too, fall into the same pit. Approach people with a humble attitude, with prayer and a spirit of gentleness.

3. *Will the confrontation mend a severed relationship?* Matthew 5 and 18 both tell us to take the initiative to mend a rupture if someone has sinned against us or holds a grudge against us. Most people might say, "I didn't do anything wrong; let them apologize to me." But God wants us to initiate reconciliation. If a relationship has been damaged in any way and is not quickly repaired, we need to be the peacemakers by purposely talking to the other person in an effort to reconcile.

My family lives in Chicago and I live in Pennsylvania, so

holidays are especially difficult. I learned to deal with my loneliness by inviting everybody from the church who didn't have a place to go to come to my house for Thanksgiving, Christmas, New Year's Eve, and Labor Day. Sharon, a friend of mine, was a regular at our parties and I was always glad to have her, but after a while I began to notice that Sharon never invited me to her house. Now I'm embarrassed to admit it, but I began to feel a little resentful and then I began to wonder if she even liked me. *Maybe Sharon's just using me to get a free meal or to have someplace to go for the holidays,* I thought to myself. Before long I avoided her, because I certainly wasn't going to confront her with a question like, "Why haven't you invited me for dinner?"

This worked for a couple of months, but my resentment grew and God started prodding me, saying, "I want you to talk to her." So finally I made a deal with Him. I would talk to Sharon if He made it very obvious and very easy. Well, before long we ran into each other at church. She was coming up a staircase and I was going down. I took that as God's cue to speak to her.

"Sharon, can we talk?" I asked.

"Sure," she said, "what's on your mind?"

Immediately tears welled up in my eyes and I blurted, "Sharon, this is so hard for me to say, but why haven't you invited me over for dinner?"

Stunned, Sharon answered, "I just don't do dinners. I never have anybody over. My house is so small, I don't like to cook, and I could never make anything as nice or as fancy as you, Leslie. I feel so inferior and insecure about those kinds of things. I never entertain."

As it turns out, God was working not just in my life, but in Sharon's life, too, about her insecurity and self-consciousness that absolutely ruled everything she did. As a result of feeling uncomfortable about her house and her cooking abilities, she had failed to love me and many others as her friends when she neglected to return the gift of hospitality. By the way, Sharon eventually did have me over for dinner and she did a fine job. But it was good for both of us to talk about this issue because it brought about a true peaceful resolution to our wounded relationship.

HOW WOMEN HANDLE CONFLICT

A while ago I asked some women from my church how they react to conflict at church, work, home, or among their friends. Interestingly, all of the women I surveyed said they felt uneasy about conflict, wondering if they should speak up or let it pass. Why do we find it even more difficult than some of our Christian brothers to express our feelings when we see injustice or when someone hurts our feelings or sins against us? Why are Christian women resistant to sharing opinions and thoughts?

A revealing study conducted at Harvard University tells us a great deal about what goes on in the mind of a developing girl. This study was done by two Harvard researchers, Carol Gilligan and Lynn Brown, who surveyed over one hundred young girls over a period of several years, starting at age seven and continuing each year until the girls were eighteen. These girls all attended a private school in Ohio and each year they were asked the same set of questions: How do you disagree with others? How do you feel during a fight or in a disagreement? How do you deal with conflicts in your relationships? What do you value? What the researchers found not only startled them, but also grieved them. When these girls were young, they were outspoken about their beliefs. They weren't afraid to share what they felt even if it caused conflict. But as these young girls navigated through adolescence, they began to lose their identity. Niceness had become more important than honesty, and going along with the crowd was far more critical than conviction.

The Harvard researchers discovered that young girls knew the difference between honesty and pretending, but as they approached adolescence, they were beginning to intuit another reality called "social game playing." In this game, played by many adults, we learn to leave certain things unsaid. To speak honestly about what we think or feel is taking a risk of having our experiences denied, our feelings made fun of, or worse yet, being rejected. And when faced with the option to speak up or remain silent, the researchers found that many adolescent girls chose to be quiet, even if it meant pushing aside their own thoughts and feelings. The girls also chose to pretend that everything was fine when it really wasn't. They not only learned these lessons from their own peer group, but also from older women who subscribed to the same pattern of relating to one another.

We may think this doesn't happen to grown-up Christian women, but I beg to differ. I think a lot of us pretend. One woman put it this way when she responded to my questionnaire about conflict. She said, "These questions have made me really think about conflict. At first I assumed I didn't have any at church or work. But when I really thought about it, I realized that I don't experience conflict because I'm not totally honest with myself. I tend to go along with things and pretend things are fine when they really aren't."

In my counseling practice, numerous women say they avoid conflict because they fear alienating a relationship. They have come to believe that if people knew them, their thoughts, and their feelings, they might be laughed at, trivialized, dismissed, or rejected. As one client put it, "A little of something is better than nothing. If I let someone know what I really think and what I really feel, they might reject me and then I'd be left with nothing."

Holidays are always a time for potential conflicts. For example, rather than say, "Mom, I don't want to come home and spend Christmas morning with you and Dad anymore because I'd like to start those traditions at my own home," many women will sidestep conflict and go along with the parents' plans. We act as if everything is fine, refusing to share what we really think or feel, all because we want to avoid possible trouble and personal rejection. Unfortunately, women have been taught, sometimes by our mothers and oftentimes by each other, to disregard our feelings, our intuitions, and our thoughts in order to maintain peace.

At my home I have a garden where I planted some orange tiger lilies underneath the overhang of my garage before I realized that they would not get much sun there. Each year, I'm amused to watch the lilies grow horizontally rather than vertically as they stretch their stems to find a little bit of sunshine. They remind me of women who are people-pleasers, who are always looking for other people to approve or desire them. They lean in the direction of their nourishment or inspiration and bend in unnatural and unhealthy positions, damaging the person God intended them to be. The truth is, God doesn't want us to be "other-centered" women; He wants us to be God-centered women.

He wants us to receive our nourishment and strength from Him so that when other people disagree with us we aren't so ruffled. God wants us to have the freedom to be who we really are.

THE ART OF CONFRONTATION

So how do we confront when it's necessary? What should we do? As Queen Ester did, the first thing we need to do is pray. We need to turn the situation over to God and ask Him for the best possible resolution.

The second thing we may have to do is consult other godly people who will help us develop a plan. Please don't use this as an opportunity to gossip about the other person. In fact, it would be better not to mention the other person's name. But it's especially helpful to ask for some godly advice if a situation is potentially explosive.

Third, choose the right time and place to confront someone. When Esther asked to speak to the king, she invited him to dinner. But somehow she knew the timing wasn't quite right, so she invited him again the next night. Timing is critical. Don't talk to someone when they're tired or in a bad mood, or when we haven't preplanned the moment to have enough time to talk.

Always try to confront in person if at all possible. An anonymous letter is not the way to speak the truth in love. I received an anonymous letter once, and though the person had some good points, I would have liked to talk to them in person. If you absolutely must write, include your name so they can get back to you. A peaceful resolution should be the goal. Plan your words. As a writer, I know it is difficult to communicate what you really want to say the first time around. Words must be chosen carefully. If we're reckless with them, it's like throwing gasoline on a fire, causing incredible damage to an already shaky relationship. Make sure that you're truthful, but loving and gracious.

Keep the other person's best interest in mind when you talk to them. Most of all, seek to restore the relationship. While you're talking, watch your nonverbal cues. What we say with our words is only 7 percent of what is communicated. Our tone and body language comprise the remainder. People pay much more attention to how you look and what you sound like when you speak than what you actually say. When you confront someone, make sure your voice, your body, and your words all communicate the same sentiment, which should be, "I love you, I care about this rupture in our relationship, and I want it to be restored."

Ask for their response and listen carefully to what they have to say. Carefully consider their point of view.

Jesus' greatest mission on this earth was reconciliation—reconciling sinners to Himself. But reconciliation requires a response. We may try to enact peace but fail to get the response we had hoped for. In Romans 12, the apostle Paul tells us to do all we can in our power to bring about peace. But it does not rest on our shoulders alone. Though our job is to pursue peace, to speak the truth in love, and to pray for our friends and enemies, we must ultimately trust Christ with the outcome. If we can remember to do that, then we will become true peacemakers who glorify God.

ABOUT THE AUTHOR

With more than twenty years' experience, Leslie Vernick is a respected and trusted clinical social worker who has her own private counseling practice. She is a guest lecturer at Westminster Seminary, and an author and popular conference speaker who loves teaching people how to move their faith from head knowledge to heart-based trust.

VERSES THAT INSPIRE

Be of one mind, live in peace. And the God of love and peace will be with you. (2 Corinthians 13:11)

Finally, all of you, live in harmony with one another; be sympathetic, love as brothers, be compassionate and humble. (1 Peter 3:8)

But avoid foolish controversies and genealogies and strife and disputes about the law, because these are unprofitable and useless. (Titus 3:9)

Do not repay anyone evil for evil. Be careful to do what is right in the eyes of everybody. If it is possible, as far as it depends on you, live at peace with everyone. (Romans 12:17)

Everyone should be quick to listen, slow to speak and slow to become angry. (James 1:19)

Overcoming Depression

CATHERINE HART WEBER

Why are you so downcast, O my soul, my inner self?
Why are you so disturbed and disquieted within me?
I choose to put my hope in you, God, to wait expectantly for you,
and I will still praise You, my help, my Savior and my God.
O my God, my life is downcast within me,
and it is more than I can bear; therefore I will remember you!
—PRAYER INSPIRED BY PSALM 42:5–6

One in five women reading this book is at risk for experiencing a period of depression in her lifetime. If you are not depressed right now, you might know someone who is and needs help and healing from depression. The truth is, you or your loved ones don't have to live with the pain of depression and suffer alone. Just toughing it out and not taking care of yourself will not help you "snap out of it." There is hope and healing and practical help for overcoming depression. If you are feeling hopeless or incurable, that in itself is a symptom of depression. Let me encourage you that God is with you during this dark time, although it may not feel like it. He loves you dearly and understands your pain.

God has designed us to have the capacity to experience depression. While severe depression can be caused by a biological imbalance, less severe situational depressions can be purposeful, or a natural response to loss. Just as pain is important for the survival of the body because it alerts us to harm and disease, depression tells us that something is out of order in our life—body, mind, emotions, spirit, relationships.

Regardless of the cause of depression, God provides a variety of resources for healing. Through hope in Christ, the power of His Word and Holy Spirit, and the current benefits of research and medical advances, depression can almost always be treated successfully with psychotherapy, medication, or a combination of both, as well as other alternative integrative interventions.

UNDERSTANDING DEPRESSION

Unfortunately, many women suffer needlessly because they either don't recognize the symptoms of depression or they are not correctly diagnosed and treated properly. Since there are no biological tests for depression, the diagnosis is usually a matter of recognizing a cluster of symptoms. The most recognizable symptom of clinical depression is an abnormal change in mood, which explains the term "mood or affective disorder." Depression is not always limited to mood changes and is therefore considered a whole-person disorder, since the body, mind, emotions, relationships, and spirituality are affected.

Following many years of scientific research, we now know that the underlying causes of depression—whether depression is classified as an illness, disease, disorder, or syndrome—are complexly interrelated and the symptoms include a wide variety of discomforts in every area of life. The origins stem from your body, genes, temperament, pattern of thinking, way of handling emotions, family history, relationships, and past and present experience. It is truly a whole-body, whole-person disorder, and in order for treatment to be effective, it must also be comprehensive, involving a comprehensive treatment plan, which may include antidepressant medications, counseling, attention to your own self-care, and developing a healthy lifestyle.

DEPRESSION FACTS

To actively participate in recovery, it is important to be educated about depression. By learning more about the topic and how the healing process works, you will gain a stronger sense of control and empowerment to deal with overcoming depression. So, to provide you perspective on the topic, let's begin by covering some of the current basic facts about depression.

- According to the National Institute of Mental Health, current estimates say the epidemic of major depression affects approximately 10 percent of the population, or over twenty million people annually.

- Studies show an increase of depression with each new generation. Those born after 1940—the baby boomer generation—are ten times more likely to suffer from depression.

- By the year 2020, depression is predicted to be the greatest disability worldwide.

- Women are more than twice as likely as men to experience major depression, and depression is a greater threat to a woman's social and physical functioning than serious medical conditions such as hypertension, diabetes, or arthritis.

- Depression in women crosses all racial and ethnic lines, and all educational and economic barriers to become a significant cause of both disability and loss of income for women of all ages.

- Consequences of depression are pain and suffering, disability, significant loss of income, an increased risk of suicide, morbidity from medical illness, risk of poor self-care, and reduced adherence to medical regimes.

- Women who suffer with depression often struggle with chronic stress and anxiety as well.

- Although depression tends to recur for many women, most depressions are treatable. The earlier treatment begins, the less severe the depression and less likely to recur.

- Mild to moderate depression is by far the most common form of mental disease, which is often misdiagnosed and primarily treated by medical doctors. Yet only about 30 percent of those suffering from depression seek help. Of those who do seek treatment, only half are accurately diagnosed —and only about 20 percent of those people are treated properly. Additionally, there are other barriers that can also obstruct women from receiving adequate treatment, so a significantly small number of women are actually getting the help they need!

When a woman is depressed, the family and especially the children are also impacted. If she is the primary caregiver in the family, the disease touches the lives of those around her, adversely affecting the family structure in a profound way. For every depressed woman, at least three other lives are significantly impacted. Children of depressed parents have an increased risk for major depressive disorders and anxiety disorders. They show poorer overall functioning, as well as an increased risk of general medical problems and psychiatric hospitalizations. This data highlights the importance of getting help for depression as early as possible, as well as support for the family during the healing process.

RECOGNIZING DEPRESSION

Depression goes back to the earliest times, with several examples even in Scripture. In Psalm 51, King David writes of his despair caused by unconfessed sin and difficult circumstances, which led to a groaning in his soul and a loss of strength. God used depression to gain Nehemiah's attention in order to do His work of rebuilding Jerusalem (Nehemiah 1:3–4). Job experienced so much pain and loss that he cursed the day he was born (Job 3). Elijah was so depressed after a great victory that he wanted to die (1 Kings 19:1–18).

Over the years, with the advances of science and medicine, we have come to a much better understanding of the origins and treatment of depression, and we continue to learn more every day.

TYPES OF DEPRESSION

Unipolar—symptoms lasting for more than two weeks.

Bipolar—depression that includes cycles of mania.

Dysthymia—long-term, chronic depression. Symptoms are usually mild and last for at least two years without a break for more than two months.

Atypical depression—chronic depression with other symptoms such as excessive fatigue, oversleeping, and overeating.

Seasonal depression—seasonal affective disorder (SAD). Onset is associated with a certain time of the year or insufficient sunlight.

Psychotic depression—severe depression accompanied by delusions or hallucinations, requiring immediate psychiatric care.

Hormonal depressions—premenstrual dysphoric disorder

(PMDD), premenstrual syndrome (PMS), postpartum depression, and perimenopausal depression. These depressions correlate with a drop in estrogen levels and often require medical or hormonal therapy in addition to antidepressants.

Posttraumatic stress disorder (PTSD)—depression that can occur after exposure to a traumatic life-threatening experience.

Masked depression—This is not formally recognized in the diagnostic manual; however, this term acknowledges what often occurs when someone suffers from depression and is not aware of it, "masking" it behind some other problem or activity such as physical problems, excessive working, or anger.

SYMPTOMS OF DEPRESSION

- You're forgetful, and it's very difficult to concentrate on anything.
- You feel as though you're drowning or suffocating.
- You're agitated, jumpy, anxious, and worried much of the time.

- Your home is a mess—laundry and dishes pile up, mail is unopened, etc.
- You hope you don't run into anyone you know while you're out.
- You let yourself go. You fail to take good care of yourself, and you don't care.
- You lose interest in the things you used to like, including sex.
- Things just seem "off" or "wrong" in your life.
- You have a lot of discomfort, including aches and pains in your body.

What's wrong? These are all typical and atypical symptoms of depression. Somewhere out of all the pain of depression, there has to be a message. The message could come out of nowhere, signaling to you that something is not right. Or it could be ongoing, alerting you to stop and think about your life and make some changes. It helps, therefore, to pause and ask yourself, "What is this depression telling me? What are the best treatment options?"

Part of the reason that clinical depression affects women

more than men is that they often fail to recognize signs early on, or they think they should be able to "make themselves feel better" or "snap out of it." This prevents many women from identifying depression, heeding the warnings, and obtaining the treatment needed before depression takes a dramatic hold on their lives.

The sooner you get treatment, the less severe your symptoms will be, the faster you'll recover, and the less chance there is for recurrence. Don't just rely on your primary physician to identify your symptoms as depression, but ask for a second opinion if you can, as well as a referral for a full evaluation from a psychologist or psychiatrist. The key to getting correct diagnoses for depression is to recognize that the disease impacts every area of life, and symptoms might not appear as "typical" depression. Here is a checklist of possible symptoms associated with depression:

Physical Symptoms

- Chronic aches and pains that don't respond to treatment, such as headaches; constipation; pain in the back, stomach, joints, muscles, or chest

- Appetite and weight changes
- Sleep disturbances—inability to sleep, tossing and turning, not being able to get back to sleep, irregular sleep patterns, sleeping too much
- Constant fatigue or loss of energy
- Slow, soft speech
- Anxiety or panic attacks

Mental Symptoms

- Difficulty in concentrating, remembering things, making decisions, and thinking clearly
- Obsessing over negative experiences or thoughts
- Low self-esteem
- Recurrent thoughts of suicide or death
- Attitude of: "What difference does it make?"

Emotional/ Mood Symptoms

- Depressed mood—feelings of helplessness, worthlessness, sadness, irritability, and pessimism for most of the day

- Excessive crying or an inability to cry or express emotion
- Feelings of worthlessness, hopelessness, inappropriate guilt, or blaming yourself for your problems
- Loss of interest in previously pleasurable activities; inability to enjoy usual hobbies or activities, including sex
- Unresolved grief and loss issues

Behavioral Symptoms

- Observable restlessness, irritability, or decreased activity
- Substance abuse such as alcohol or drugs
- Suicide attempts
- Decreased performance at work or school
- Social withdrawal—refusal to go out and see friends; avoidance of friends
- Avoidance of situations that could cause responsibility or failure
- Dislike of crowds
- Difficulty getting along with others

DEPRESSION RISK FACTORS AND CAUSES

Given all the possible symptoms that signal depression, what can this syndrome tell you about yourself? Causes of depression can be complex and multifaceted. Trying to understand the origins of depression can in many ways be similar to trying to understand the complexity of an illness like heart disease, diabetes, or cancer. Depression is neither all in your head nor all in your body. It is not a sign of personal weakness, nor is it a condition that you can overcome just by pulling yourself together. Depression is the natural consequence of physical and situational causes.

There are many factors that can predispose a woman to depression, and knowing what they are is the first step in prevention and treatment. It could be just one issue, or there could be a few, interrelated and overlapping. Review the following list and see if there are any themes with which you identify or current events that may become triggers for depression.

Psychological Risk Factors

- Early developmental struggles
- Mothers of young children
- Teenage girls
- The pursuit of thinness
- Chronic strain and stress
- Baby boomers and other generational changes
- Urban dwellers
- Immigrants
- Poverty and minority status
- The elderly
- Alcohol, substance, and sexual addictions

Biological Risk Factors

- Imbalance of brain chemical messengers
- Family history of depression
- Reproductive hormones
- Hormonal drugs and medications
- Medical conditions
- Chronic illness, disability, and coexistent illness

Relationship Risk Factors

- Sexual and physical abuse
- Marriage and children
- Social and role pressures
- Low self-esteem
- Singleness and single-parenting
- Attachment losses

Mental and Cognitive Risk Factors

- Personality styles and psychological makeup (pessimistic, melancholy)
- Learned helplessness or no sense of control
- Rumination

Other Risk Factors for Depression

- Pain and challenges in your life
- Reaction to circumstances in one's life
- Continuous struggles
- Past traumas and losses

WHY DO WOMEN BECOME DEPRESSED MORE THAN MEN?

In addition to the triggers listed above, recent studies confirm that the most prominent causes of depression among women worldwide can be clustered into the following categories:

1. *Hormones.* Hormones play a huge role in the life of a woman, starting at puberty, childbirth, PMS, PMDD, post-partum blues, postpartum depression, postpartum psychosis, perimenopause, menopause, and beyond. It appears that in many ways, a woman's brain chemistry interacts with repro-ductive hormones. When there is a change in one, this can impact her other systems. For example, pregnancy and deliv-ery produce dramatic changes in estrogen and progesterone levels, as well as changes in the HPG axis, which may be the underlying cause of postpartum depression. Mothers-to-be need to be aware of the risks of depression at this stage and recognize the symptoms early on, in order to prevent and treat it.

2. *Genetic Links.* Recent data confirms that major depres-sion can cluster in families who have a parent or sibling with

this disorder. Women possess an interaction of genetic, hormonal, and experiential factors that heighten their risk for depression.

3. *Life Stress.* Studies show that more than 80 percent of women experiencing major depression underwent an adverse life event. Women are more likely to experience depression in response to a stressful life situation and ongoing stress such as work overload. Stress and anxiety often go hand-in-hand with depression in women.

4. *Psychological and Cognitive Factors.* Due to social and cultural factors, women are less inclined than men to act on their problems, yet more inclined to dwell on them. Women tend to act inwardly, repetitively and passively focusing on symptoms of distress and their possible causes and consequences. This is known as ruminative thinking. The cycle of stress, negative thinking, and emotions actually creates more stress and is also associated with longer and more severe episodes of depression.

5. *Quality of Relationships.* Recent research demonstrates that a woman's relationships are more paramount to her self-concept than those of men. Women are also more likely to

experience stress in response to adverse events affecting the lives of others and place their needs secondary to those in distress. In unhappy marriages, women are three times as likely as men to be depressed. Women's risk of depressive symptoms and demoralization is higher among mothers of young children and increases with the number of children in the house.

6. *Trauma.* Traumatic events such as childhood sexual abuse, physical and mental abuse, adult sexual assault, terrorism, male partner violence, and physical illness can also lead to depression. Sexual and physical abuse can result in loss of self-esteem and self-worth, putting women at risk for depression. In life-threatening situations, women are at risk for posttraumatic stress disorder.

My purpose in sharing this information is to give you some insight into the possible causes of depression. None of the risk factors I have described is insurmountable. You might not feel very hopeful right now, but take heart. Start with what you learn in this chapter, then reach out for help from a friend, pastor, or professional counselor. Above all, *continue in a spirit of prayer.* Lean as hard as you can on God for His empowerment in your life. He has promised to walk with you through life's darkest moments: "I will never leave you nor forsake you" (Joshua 1:5). He will be with you all the way through the valley, providing you with caring, helpful resources to accomplish your healing (Psalm 23).

GETTING HELP TO HEAL DEPRESSION

If you or someone you know is experiencing depression, don't let neglect or hindrances prevent you from getting the needed treatment for overcoming depression. It is very important not to let depression go on for too long, and not to struggle through it alone. Depression is treatable, but you will need the support of others, as well as the resources available for recovery. There is no need to continue suffering alone. Here are some guidelines to get started.

TREATMENT RECOMMENDATIONS

If you've noticed signs of depression in yourself or someone you know, the first priority is a full and thorough physical examination to rule out any possible underlying medical causes or illnesses. Let the doctor know if you are on any prescription medications or nonprescription substances, since these could contribute to your depression.

Once any physical disorders and illnesses have been ruled out, a full psychological evaluation by a counselor or psychiatrist is the next step. A clear understanding of all possible underlying causes of depression is imperative to help direct your doctor, counselor, and psychiatrist toward the most effective short-term and long-term treatment.

I realize that this might be difficult for some women. There has been a stigma associated with depression, counseling, and antidepressant medication that has taken an unfortunate toll on women. This could be contributing to unnecessary prolonged pain, preventing you from getting the practical help you need. Remember, God has created us with the capacity for depression, and you are not a failure spiritually or mentally if you are not able to overcome it yourself. For a complete recovery, you will need support from those around you and practical resources that God has provided through the advancements of counseling and medicine.

Keep in mind, depression serves a purpose: It can be an opportunity for healing or an indicator that something is out of order in your life. You wouldn't be inattentive to treatment if you had another concern, like diabetes or heart disease. Depression is no different. Ask God to calm your fears and misconceptions, and to help you be open to the healing resources He wants to make available to you. God has promises you, "Do not fear, for I am with you; do not be dismayed, for I am your God. I will strengthen you and help you; I will uphold you with my righteous right hand" (Isaiah 41:10).

Psychotherapy

God intended us to have meaningful connections with others, and He gave us His gifts to help us help one another. "Let us therefore come boldly to the throne of grace, that we may obtain mercy and find grace to help in time of need" (Hebrews 4:16 NKJV). For this reason, counseling could very well be a part of His provision to bring healing and recovery to your life. A counselor is someone who is trained to create a safe place for you in order to explore the complexities of your life, the underlying causes of your depression, and how that depression relates to and impacts your life and relationships. Professional counseling provides reliable, consistent, uninterrupted time for you to be heard and valued. This can also be a growing place to help you achieve clarity. Counseling is a partnership, first with God, and then with your counselor.

Studies show that psychotherapy is very useful in preventing relapse or recurrence of major depression in women who have been successfully treated with antidepressants. Counseling alone can be very helpful in resolving underlying causes of depression if antidepressants are not needed. Interpersonal and cognitive behavioral therapy have been shown to have a lasting effect, as well as other counseling styles such as structured behavioral marital and family therapies, which are also very helpful in treating families.

Antidepressant Medications

There is a great deal of misunderstanding—and even fear—surrounding the use of antidepressant medication. Resistance toward appropriate use of antidepressants is unjustified once you understand the brain and how it can function more appropriately with specific medications. Antidepressants aren't mind-altering or addictive medications; they work by helping the brain do what it was designed to do, only more efficiently. They help by increasing at least two important chemical messengers in the brain, neurotransmitters, which become depleted when depressed. These messengers are norepinephrine (NE) and serotonin (5HT). These and other biochemical reactions affect the command center of the brain so that the brain and body can function normally. This, in turn, relieves depression symptoms by improving mood and decreasing negative thinking.

There are many highly advanced antidepressants now available, with fewer and fewer side effects. No one medication is perfect for everyone, and it might take a process of experimenting to find the most effective medication for you, with the fewest side effects. So if your counselor or doctor recommends an antidepressant, I encourage you to be open and patient. Ask God for peace in receiving His provision for healing. Psalm 30:1–2 says: "I will exalt you, O LORD, for you lifted me out of the depths and did not let my enemies gloat over me. O LORD my God, I called to you for help and you healed me." Many women have found the recovery they had been praying for through this type of antidepressant treatment.

There is no "magic pill" to solve all depression. Unless the origin is biologically based, it is really important to be in counseling to resolve the underlying cause of depression. In fact, research demonstrates that antidepressant medication along with counseling offers the most effective long-term results.

Use Complementary Therapies Wisely

About 30 percent of those taking antidepressants do not respond to this form of treatment or have adverse reactions. For these women, herbs, natural substances, and other forms of treatment are appealing and often necessary. Since women make up over 65 percent of the population who purchase natural products, you might have already tried some of them.

Complementary medicine and lifestyle therapies such as spirit/mind/body approaches can allow you to take an active role in your own life and health and minimize difficult side effects caused by conventional medical regimes. Prayer, meditation, relational support, nutritional wellness, exercise, and massage all promote health in general, as well as build resistance and resilience to depression and many illnesses.

On the other hand, some pharmacological, herbal, and vitamin supplementation can be harmful when overdosed or mixed with other medications. Herbs such as St. John's wort, kava, ginkgo biloba, and valerian are God's natural pharmaceuticals, and they must be used wisely. Just because a substance or regime is "natural" doesn't mean you shouldn't take necessary precautions. Do your homework. Ask your doctor or other healthcare professional who is knowledgeable about complimentary medicine to point out areas of concern. Be sure to avoid using any other substances while taking medication unless you first check with your doctor or pharmacist.

STRATEGIES FOR OVERCOMING DEPRESSION

Let me encourage you that many other women have successfully ventured on the journey to recovery and you can too. Here are some approaches to consider as you lay a foundation for practical lifestyle strategies.

1. *Acknowledge your struggle with depression.* It is difficult

to know when to heed the warning signs of depression, especially in the early stages. The tendency, especially if you are busy, is to ignore them and hope they will go away. As time goes by, however, signs of depression can become more debilitating, and it becomes more difficult to tell the difference between what is "you," what is "your fault" or "weakness," and what plan of action to take to get better. If you recognize the symptoms of depression early on, it's important to admit to yourself that you are depressed and do something about it.

2. *Be honest and open with God in prayer.* Tell God about your spiritual confusion, disappointments, even anger at Him, if that is the way you feel. God's desire, and our need, is a powerful relationship with Him. Ask Him to reveal to you the underlying causes of your depression and to direct you to the right people to support you, both professionally and personally.

3. *Share your struggles with someone who will be supportive and empathetic.* Don't go through your depression alone. Once you have acknowledged your depression to yourself and God, tell one or more trusted people in your life about it as well. Women who have overcome difficult times say that the connections they have with other women were crucial in helping

them overcome depression, as well as other life struggles.

4. *Set small goals and take small steps.* Don't try to do it all. Do what you can for the day. Break down tasks into smaller, manageable parts. You have control over the here and now. Don't expect too much of yourself too soon, or you will set yourself up for defeat. Eventually, the healing process will show changes in how you feel. But initially, take it slow, and focus on the practical behaviors of getting through the day.

5. *Remember, growing and changing happens one day at a time.* Recovery from depression takes time. It may be weeks before you see improvement, so don't get discouraged. Start with one area of your life today and take it one step at a time. Challenge any "stinking thinking" with the truth of God's Word; it will be your greatest source of strength. Meditate daily on God's truth to confront the lies of this life. Your God is there for you (Psalm 42:5).

STRATEGIES FOR WELLNESS LIVING

One of the most difficult things to do when you're depressed is to take good care of yourself. You no longer feel like participating in those activities you once enjoyed, or much of anything for that matter. If you are not careful, you can end up isolating yourself, succumbing to binge eating, not sleeping well, not exercising, getting caught in the downward spiral of negative thinking, and feeling spiritually dry and dejected by God. Investing in your own health and healing is key to your recovery, which is critical to the overall health of your family. So don't feel guilty for taking time for yourself.

In addition to securing the support and professional help you need, here are some practical basics for a healthy lifestyle that are essential to your healing as a whole person. Although these might sound simple, don't underestimate how crucial daily choices and habits are to a more effective and lasting recovery.

1. *Eat well-balanced, nutritious mini-meals,* evenly spread throughout the day. There is a connection between depression, your brain, and the food you put into your mouth.

2. *Get adequate sleep*—at least eight hours a day. One symptom often associated with depression, anxiety, and stress is sleep disturbances. Being exhausted can also lead to depression.

3. *Start exercising.* Physical activity is a mood-booster. A growing number of studies show that exercise is an effective mood-boosting, natural antidepressant treatment for depression. Brisk walking or jogging for thirty minutes a day, at least three to four times a week, can actually be as effective as medication for treating some types of depression.

4. *Reduce stress in your life.* Stress, anxiety, and depression often go hand in hand, so be mindful of chronic strains in your life, and explore the most effective techniques to help you reduce and recover from the stress in your life.

5. *Surround yourself with positives.* Learn to dispute any distorted, pessimistic beliefs you may have developed and replace them with biblical, reality-based, optimistic alternatives. On a daily basis choose to be around positive people, events, media, music, and literature.

6. *Invest in yourself.* You will have to be intentional to maintain meaningful activities in your life, such as getting together with friends, enjoying hobbies, going places, and having fun.

7. *Invest in others.* Do acts of kindness for someone else. Be available to listen or help out. When you care for yourself

as well as someone else who may need your support, it helps you maintain perspective. Besides, you'll receive a blessing in return for helping someone else in need.

Despite what might seem like great challenges and obstacles, it is possible to achieve a full recovery and to build resistance to future depression. Remember, the most effective strategy for healing is an integrative approach—treating yourself as a whole person. Utilize all the resources God can provide for your recovery—medical treatment, counseling, social support, natural therapies, prayer and Scripture, and a wellness lifestyle. Take good care of yourself, and may God bless you.

DEPRESSION SURVIVAL KIT

Pack yourself the following depression "survival kit":

A *candle* to remind you that even when you are surrounded by darkness, Christ's love is a fire that never goes out!

A *match* to remind you that sleep, relaxation, and exercise "relight your flame" when you feel burned out.

A *Band-aid* to remember that God comforts and heals, and recovery takes time!

Two paper clips joined together to remind you that connecting with God, yourself, family, friends, your community, and your Christian faith mean more than anything else.

A *pencil* to remind you to list your blessings, use a prayer journal daily, and "pencil in" time for what really matters.

An *eraser* to remind you to keep your life clean by being honest with yourself and others, asking for forgiveness, and forgiving others.

A *piece of fleece blanket* to remind you to nurture and take good care of yourself.

A *Hershey's hug or kiss* to remind you that you are loved! (But don't comfort yourself by overeating chocolate!)

Chewing gum to remind you to stick with it, to persevere in the midst of your struggles!

A *Snickers* bar to remind you that laughter is good medicine! (Okay, one piece of chocolate.)

Put all these goodies in a *clear bag* as a constant reminder that God can help you keep it all together!

ABOUT THE AUTHOR

Catherine Hart Weber is an integrative Christian counselor in private practice, specializing in relationship enrichment and personal health and growth. She is the author of several books and a conference speaker.

VERSE THAT INSPIRE

[The Lord said,] "My grace is sufficient for you,
for my power is made perfect in weakness."
(2 Corinthians 12:9)

Do not fear, for I am with you;
    do not be dismayed, for I am your God.
I will strengthen you and help you;
    I will uphold you with my righteous right hand.
(Isaiah 41:10)

God is our refuge and strength, an ever-present
help in trouble. (Psalm 46:1)

The LORD will hear when I call to him.
(Psalm 4:3)

Do not let your hearts be troubled. Trust in God;
trust also in me. (John 14:1)

Dealing with Life's Changes

❧

DR. JOSEPH AND MARY ANN MAYO

Satisfy us in the morning with your unfailing love,
that we may sing for joy and be glad all our days.
—PSALM 90:14

Aging is a blessing from God, even though many of us don't think so as the next birthday lies in wait. We are shocked at the sudden death of a young person who is tragically killed in a car accident or whose life is cut short by leukemia, since most of us adhere to the concept that the old are supposed to die, not the young. But the equation of "old = death" leaves out a lot of living. It is no wonder that we remain uncomfortable with growing old if dying is all we associate with it. I (Mary Ann) have never lied about my age but, I confess, I never thought of myself as old until my sixtieth birthday. Denying getting older suggests that something is wrong with being more experienced, more knowledgeable, and hopefully more spiritual. Older should translate into being wiser, simpler, and less worldly all at the same time.

Denying age is not the solution to facing getting older. The Bible calls on us to think of ourselves realistically (Romans 12:4). When it comes to aging, this is a concept not embraced by many. But to look only at the dark side—"Oh, aging is just being infirm or over the hill," or "I have no time left for creative expression"—ignores the truth. Scripture reminds us that young people take pride in their strength, but the gray hairs of wisdom are even more beautiful (Proverbs 20:29). Job asks the rhetorical questions, "Is not wisdom found among the aged? Does not long life bring understanding?" (Job 12:12). God's plan was for the aged to remain a vital part of the community. Bottom line, whether we accept God's design or not, and whether we enter our "golden years" kicking and screaming or with anticipation and excitement, we cannot escape the inevitable: We will get old.

Acceptance of such a truth does not eliminate mixed feelings about facing the task of getting older. Many people struggle because aging means they must accept that changes have to be made. Making changes can be difficult. People agonize over the fact that things will be different. But there is no avoiding the necessity of change. A truth of change, however, is that acceptance comes when a woman allows herself to grieve what must be left behind, and perhaps even what new things must take its place. Even when there is wholehearted enthusiasm for making changes, grieving is part of the process. It should not be a surprise that the midlife woman, with all her physical and social changes, finds she has much to grieve.

For example, just when a woman's body signals she must begin her struggle with her personal journey of aging, chances are she must simultaneously confront the deteriorating health of her parents, children leaving home, a career change or job stagnation or, as in Dr. Mayo's and my situation, illness. His unexpected heart attack forced us to re-prioritize and restructure our lives as focused individuals and as a couple. The so-called "golden years" frequently force us to evaluate and accept some serious responsibilities. The more reevaluation and planning we do before a crisis occurs, the greater the chance that it will be handled well.

An honest, timely appraisal is in order. It must begin with an overview of the condition of mind, body, and spirit. Film star Brigitte Bardot had the right idea. She once said, "It is so sad to grow old, but it is so nice to ripen." Her statement says much about the choices we make as we age and the attitude we hold toward getting older. It is far from a message of despair. It is not defining aging in terms of shriveling up or diminishing.

Ripening is the perfect metaphor for describing quality aging. Think about it. Unripe fruit may be nourishing, but ripe fruit by contrast supplies more than just food for the body. It is attractive. Its rich, vibrant colors and aromatic perfume draws us to it. We want to pick it up and partake of its lushness and juiciness.

How do we nurture a "ripe-fruit" persona? How do we gracefully move from one stage to another? Let's examine the ripening process.

R stands for reprioritizing. A midlife woman is beginning the last one-third of her life. She is not at the end of her life. What remains undone? What is left that must be negated or begun? What needs attending to immediately? What legacy will be left behind?

I is for instituting new health habits like adding nutritional supplements and drinking green tea.

P stands for pacing oneself so that exercise and reduction of stress become priorities.

E is for evaluating health in order to make informed decisions about individual needs. Knowing one's baseline health is essential to proceed.

N is for nutrition. A diet that results in a ripening maturity requires intelligent evaluation of what is used for nourishment of both body and soul.

REFRAMING OUR CONCEPT OF AGING

Thinking of aging as ripening is a new concept for many. When we alter our traditional way of seeing something and perceive it in a new way, we are "reframing." Seeing aging positively requires reframing. Reframing is also appropriate when our goal is to insure our relationships will "ripen" into a richness that surpasses the ordinary. We start reframing by honestly looking at the roles we have traditionally played.

For example, it is not uncommon for a woman to have lived as if everything depended on her. There's even a name for such behavior: It's been called the "ruler of the roost syndrome." Any woman who enters midlife having been the ruler of her roost may find herself beginning the aging process justifiably tired. In fact, should you be such a woman, you may be looking at your life

Any woman who enters midlife having been the ruler of her roost may find herself beginning the aging process justifiably tired.

and saying, "I can't do this anymore. I did ten things in ten minutes before, but not anymore. What's more, I don't want to do it either!"

If that sounds familiar, you need reframing. Meeting everyone's demands meant that something in your life had to give. Often it was things like sleep or good nutrition, or perhaps a few personal dreams and desires about what *you* wanted to do—like painting or playing the piano. Perhaps your spiritual life suffered while you were ruler of the roost. It may certainly be new for you to think beyond being "ruler" or beyond just surviving, but if you believe that contentment and optimal health are the defining goals of aging well, then you really have no choice but to make the necessary changes.

Where do you begin? First of all, there is good news: Even small goals can result in big changes. They also allow for adjustments and course corrections. The question that is really being asked is, "How can I treat myself better?" Most women could use more rest, more quiet time, less responsibility, and a more structured plan for their health. When menopause symptoms signal the "change of life" has begun, the process of reprioritization takes on a new urgency. The stressors that accompany menopause may complicate its course, but they also provide the impetus for change.

MENOPAUSE AS A NEW BEGINNING

Menopause is one of the few things that all women share in common. It's a natural process signaled by changes in the reproductive hormones estrogen, progesterone, and to some degree, testosterone. Menopause is a journey that takes a number of years, rather than being a specific moment or some memorable day when a switch is thrown that opens the floodgates to old age. Technically, a post-menopausal woman no longer has viable eggs in her ovaries and has not had a period for a year.

A woman's genetic makeup, her lifestyle, and her health going into menopause will determine what her experience will be. The time before periods actually stop—perimeno-pause—can be more bothersome for many women than post-menopause because the hormone levels fluctuate errati-cally. The body continues to produce hormones, but changes the ratio of one hormone to another. There are women who really wonder what everybody else is talking about when they hear complaints about menopausal issues. They are the lucky one-third who can honestly say, "Menopause? It was easy; no problem at all. " Another one-third will have bothersome symptoms off and on—maybe for weeks or for months—and they wonder, "What's happening? Things are different." The remaining one-third of women go for weeks or even years being miserable.

Occasionally young women experience "premature" menopause. They may have a medical condition or treatment that destroyed their ovarian function. Or they were simply born without an adequate number of eggs in the ovaries to sustain the number of cycles needed to reach the normal age of menopause. The menopause journey can begin very early in some women (as early as age thirty-seven), with subtle changes such as occasional hot flashes and irregular periods. These may be signals that her body is preparing for menopause—a stage called premenopause. A woman is said to be "perimenopausal" approximately five years before the last menstrual period. Symptoms may intensify and become more regular. Many women find this time confusing and fail to connect the symptoms with menopause because they may continue to have regular periods. Often a woman's doctor declares she is "too young" to be menopausal and reinforces that her health issues are not related to hormonal changes. Early menopause is more common among women who smoke and those who have had a hysterectomy. A hysterectomy, even when the ovaries remain, can negatively affect the ovarian blood supply and contribute to early menopause. The point is, a woman who has had a hysterectomy and feels her symptoms suggest menopause might very well be menopausal and should insist on the appropriate tests to determine her hormone levels.

There is a tendency among women to think that once their periods have stopped they no longer need to be concerned about their health: *I've made it through menopause. I don't need any kind of medical intervention; I don't even have to go to the doctor anymore.* In fact, after periods stop, other health issues can become serious concerns—osteoporosis, heart disease, Alzheimer's, and diabetes among them.

SIGNS AND SYMPTOMS OF MENOPAUSE

The number one symptom of menopause is irregular periods. A majority (72 percent) of women find periods gradually lighten and finally stop. Some women suffer from very irregular and/or heavy periods, while a lucky few simply and suddenly stop having periods. The second most common symptom involves temperature control: hot flashes, cold flashes, and night sweats. These fluctuations can last a few weeks or (for an unfortunate few) for years, and can range from a mild annoyance to severe discomfort. Night sweats and hot flashes often disrupt sleep patterns or cause sleeplessness.

While most women report few changes in sexual function, decreases in estrogen may result in diminished sexual desire or cause vaginal pain with intercourse due to a reduction of lubrication. Painful intercourse and problems with leaky urine can both be corrected by the addition of natural or pharmaceutical estrogen, progesterone, or testosterone cream ordered by a physician and applied directly into the vagina. Very little, if any, hormone makes its way into the bloodstream. It works directly at the source of irritation by building up the surrounding tissue. The increased blood supply in the area helps repair the area that aids in urinary control, without need of surgery. Complaints of dry skin and hair are common.

For some women, anxiety, depression, and mood swings are the worst symptoms of changing hormones. A sense of hopelessness, anger, and dissatisfaction makes life miserable for the woman and sometimes for those who live with her. Loss of memory, fuzzy thinking, or the inability to recall words can be frustrating, raising fears of Alzheimer's. Joint and bone pain are also frequent complaints.

Risk Factors after Menopause

While signs and symptoms of menopause are bothersome and can affect the quality of a woman's life, the real risks are much more serious. Symptoms can be so annoying a woman may feel she is going crazy, but it is risk factors that kill. Cardiovascular disease, Alzheimer's, osteoporosis, diabetes, and colon cancer all increase post-menopausally. Deciding what, if anything, needs to be done about these risks depends on a woman's unique health history. A full medical examination and evaluation is necessary to understand the seriousness of the risk for each individual. Knowing the risk exists provides a clue to necessary interventions and making wise choices for treatment should they be necessary.

While most women are well aware that menopause ushers in changes to their lifestyle, few are realistic about the health risks they face. A recent Gallup Poll showed that 69 percent of women fear dying from cancer and 49 percent of these specifically fear breast cancer. But the reality is that heart disease is a woman's greatest risk. Approximately 450,000 women die of heart disease annually compared to 42,000 who die of breast cancer. In fact, all the gynecological cancers combined do not come close to the death rate from cardiovascular disease. Women develop an increased risk for heart disease after menopause because they no longer have estrogen to protect cardiovascular function.

Wise decisions about improving and maintaining health cannot be made without good information. To help you remember what information you need to gather, think of the acrostic FABLL.

"FA" stands for family history. It is particularly important to know whether or not your parents had heart disease; in particular: your mother before age sixty-four, your father before age fifty-five. When Dr. Mayo had his heart attack, he was baffled as to why it happened: "I had always been Mr. Healthy. I stayed thin. I exercised a lot. I took nutritional supplements. I ate the proper foods. And then I had the heart attack. But what I failed to take into consideration was the power of my genes. My father had a heart attack at sixty-three."

It is equally important to consider genetic factors for osteo-porosis. The disease may not have been officially diagnosed, but you may be aware of clues—a grandmother with a "hump" back or someone in the family with a history of many broken bones. Risk is increased if you are Asian, fair-skinned, or have a history of an eating disorder or steroid use (perhaps needed for asthma). Question also whether any family members suffered from Alzheimer's, diabetes, or colon cancer. While you are at it, consider your own medical history. Recall medical problems, toxic exposures, and so on in your lifetime.

The "B" in FABLL stands for breast cancer history. A mother or sister who had breast cancer, particularly at a young age, is a red flag for you to be diligent with your health care and nutrition. Keep in mind, however, that most cases of breast cancer are not genetically driven.

The first "L "stands for lifestyle. Sometimes this is the most difficult aspect of taking stock of your health. Few of us women care to admit that we have not been monitoring our weight or been diligent about our exercise routine. Perhaps we have allowed stress to get the upper hand. Can you be honest about your health practices?

The final "L" in FABLL is for the laboratory tests you must have to pin down exactly what your risks are. No guessing required. Then you can know exactly where you stand regarding a number of diseases, as well your risk for future chronic problems.

It is essential to have a doctor be your partner in health. He or she can order and explain the test results needed to give a true picture of your baseline health. Armed with lab tests and bolstered by your personal and family history, you can put an individualized medical profile together that accurately reflects your health, what interventions you might need, and the direction you must take to insure an active final one-third of life. Additionally, the healthier you are when you enter menopause, the less treatment you will need. Interventions that are necessary can be minimal.

THE TRIANGLE FOR AGING WELL

There is an easy method for understanding what to do for menopause symptoms and decreasing risks associated with menopause while improving your overall health: Visualize your interventions arranged from the bottom to the top of a triangle. Your risk of side-effects, expense, and drug interactions increases as you make choices that are ever closer to the top of the triangle. The peak of the triangle includes potent pharmaceutical choices.

START AT THE BOTTOM NOT THE TOP

The base of the triangle for aging well—a healthy lifestyle—provides the foundation for optimal wellness as well as personal stability. It is the base from which medical interventions can be added should they be necessary.

A healthy foundation is dependent on good nutrition. Food is the most powerful medicine you put in your mouth. Eat a colorful variety of foods and choose organic sources when you can. Include plenty of raw and cooked vegetables, fruit, and an adequate amount of quality protein (including soy and fish). Soy builds immunity, reduces hot flashes, and protects your heart. The benefits of eating fish (protection from heart disease and arthritis), particularly salmon, at least once or twice a week should make it a "must have" on your menu. Also, forget the white stuff and add complex carbohydrates that are colorful—like brown rice, sweet potatoes, and whole wheat bread. Cook with olive oil and add a tablespoon of Barlean's Flaxseed oil (found in health food stores) to salads.

Exercise at least thirty minutes a day even if you must break it down into three, ten-minute segments. Exercising reduces hot flashes, stress, and your weight. It protects your heart, keeps your joints moving, builds strong bones, and may even be a factor in reducing breast cancer.

Schedule regular check-ups with your physician and monitor your baseline health by keeping track of cholesterol, thyroid function, homocysteine, and other blood chemistries. Between the ages of forty and fifty, have a mammogram once every two years, and then once a year after your fiftieth birthday if three consecutive tests have been normal. If you have a history of breast cancer, begin annual mammograms even earlier. Have an annual Pap smear until you are menopausal, then schedule one every two or three years. Remember, a Pap smear tests for cervical cancer, not for ovarian or uterine cancer. A pelvic exam is needed for detecting these other cancers.

Also, learn new ways to handle stress. Take up yoga for its double benefit of reducing stress and keeping joints limber. Maintain healthy relationships. Balance your spiritual life. Connect with your creative side and pursue a dream long ignored. Reconnect with nature by going outside or bringing it inside.

The significance of these baseline factors to good health is that they profoundly influence your health but are all within your control. Equally important is that they have no negative side-effects!

Following these lifestyle guidelines will help you reach a level of optimal wellness for you as an individual. It does not mean that you will never have health problems. Most people who have lived a long time have health issues that are unique to them. Genetic makeup, environmental toxic exposure, and overall wear and tear mean that "general maintenance" may not be enough. For example, many women find themselves weighing more than they should.

If you are overweight, keep your efforts to lose weight simple. Continue to eat a great variety of foods, but simply watch your portions. Don't obsess over counting calories or weighing every morsel; use your eyes instead. It is easy to see that servings in restaurants are far beyond what any human being needs at one sitting. Split your dinner with a friend or take one-half home for tomorrow's lunch!

Insure the proper balance of nutrients by using the following rule of thumb: one-third of your plate should be a protein source about the size and thickness of the palm of your hand or a deck of cards. Another one-third should be a complex carbohydrate like brown rice or whole-grain bread. The remaining one-third should be a variety of vegetables and/or a salad. The good news is that eating extra vegetables as long as you are not slathering them in sauces or butter is allowed! If you love dessert, plan for it in the balance of your overall meal. A fruit serving is always good. The rich, luscious desserts can be eaten in smaller portions.

It is a good idea to substitute some of the coffee you drink each day with green or black tea. Tea has remarkable healing powers, increases immunity, lowers the risk of heart disease and stroke, and becomes a great stress reliever, especially if you make a big deal of relaxing and taking a "tea" break.

Remember nutritional supplements as well. In 2002 the *Journal of the American Medical Association* (JAMA) declared that all Americans should be taking a multivitamin daily. The controversy is over. Take your vitamin pill! As a rule of thumb, you get what you pay for. Women should make sure that the multivitamin they take includes a good ratio of "B" vitamins to counteract stress. Folic acid, one of the "B" vitamins, is important because it lowers homocysteine, which inflames blood vessels and contributes to heart attacks. If you are taking birth control pills for perimenopause symptoms, be sure to take vitamins—birth control pills deplete vitamins. Vitamin E can be helpful in reducing hot flashes in some women and protects the heart and perhaps memory. If your Vitamin E contains selenium, you will decrease your chances of colon cancer by 40 or 50 percent.

Essential fatty acids (EFA) are critical at midlife. Your body does not make EFA, therefore, you must obtain them from food sources such as walnuts or deep-water fish such as mackerel or salmon. Essential fatty acids literally make your whole body work like a well-oiled machine, including your brain. They are instrumental in hormone balance, are known to help reduce heart attacks and strokes, and aid in the prevention or relief of arthritis and generalized dryness (including vaginal dryness). Of great importance is their ability to enhance one's own hormone function.

Because of concerns about weight control, many women avoid calcium-rich dairy products and thus become calcium-depleted. The best prevention for osteoporosis remains 1,200 milligrams of quality calcium daily in 500-milligram doses, preferably with adequate Vitamin D and magnesium provided with the calcium or in a multivitamin. In the first five years after her last menstrual period, a woman will lose 3 to 5 percent of her bone mass per year. Without adequate calcium and exercise, it is possible to lose up to 25 percent of your bone before the loss slows. Calcium is also great for the mental and physical symptoms of premenstrual syndrome (PMS). It works to reduce high blood pressure and protects the heart.

Bottom line: Midlife women should take a minimum of three or four supplements daily—a multivitamin, a calcium pill, Vitamin E, and perhaps EFA if they are not fish-eaters.

MOVING UP THE TRIANGLE

For symptoms of menopause and other issues of health that are not addressed by good lifestyle habits, additional intervention may be necessary. It is wise to start with those that will have the least possibility of negative side-effects. Botanicals and therapeutic doses of vitamins fit the bill. Should you have a reaction, it will most likely be either a rash, gastrointestinal upset, or a headache. None are life-threatening, and they disappear when the "culprit" causing the problem is discontinued.

Always buy "natural medicines" and vitamins from responsible companies that have been in business for a long time and adhere to pharmaceutical standards. Reactions caused by these types of interventions are a far cry from the serious response that can occur with prescription medicines. A recent JAMA article reported that nearly 100,000 deaths a year occur in hospitals due to problems with drugs. Non-steroid anti-inflamatory drugs (NSAIDs) such as Advil and ibuprofen are responsible for 16,000 deaths annually as a result of sudden and unexpected gastrointestinal bleeding.

In addition to botanical and nutritional supplementation, other types of complementary medical treatments such as acupuncture, acupressure, or even a massage can be helpful in relieving a variety of problems. A natural substance, glucosamine—especially when paired with chondroitin—has been shown to relieve arthritic pain and actually slow the progression of disease. Many women find that natural options combined with good lifestyle habits reduce the hot flashes, depression, insomnia, and moods that may accompany menopause.

The following are some excellent botanical substances you might consider:

Black cohosh is the chief prescription written for hot flashes in Germany. The production of herbals there is highly regulated, the standards are high, and the products are well-researched. Our only choice is to buy from a company with a good reputation. Besides relieving hot flashes with minimal if any side-effects, black cohosh has proven helpful in improving vaginal dryness and depression. Black cohosh is not estrogenic.

Chastree berry affects hormone balances and is helpful in

relieving PMS. It balances follicular stimulating hormone (FSH), which regulates ovulation.

Valerian can be used to improve sleep, and kava kava, in proper dosage, is helpful for anxiety or panic attacks.

Health food stores often have menopause formulations that contain many of these herbs plus others such as dong quai or ginseng. They can be quite helpful if they have been processed by a good company.

One of the oldest herbs, gingko biloba, has been used for over two thousand years, chiefly to aid memory. It is an antioxidant to the brain and to the heart. Most people tolerate it well, but since it is an anticoagulant, it must be balanced with other blood-thinning medications. Vitamin E, garlic, and several prescription medications have the same blood-thinning property and should be discontinued if you are soon going to have surgery. Since gingko improves blood circulation, it can be an aid for those who suffer with cold hands and feet. Additionally, gingko appears to restore sexual interest in people who take Prozac or Zoloft for depression.

Mild to moderate depression is helped by St. John's wort.

It does not work for severe depression. While it has few side-effects, like any drug it may potentially interact with other medications.

Hawthorn leaf or horse chestnut improve circulation and cholesterol balance and strengthen blood vessels. They even help prevent spider veins—broken veins that appear mainly on the legs. Many physicians also recommend a baby aspirin daily for anti-inflammatory processes and to prevent heart attack.

Since NSAIDs such as ibuprofen and Tylenol can have serious side-effects, especially in combination with alcohol, it is wise to try to gain relief from pain with natural substances such as boswellia, turmeric, ginger, or cayenne. Natural combination pain relievers are available in health food stores.

It is always wise to consult your physician with a full list of everything you are taking. Drug interactions are listed on several web sites, and so are drug depletion scales. Many prescription medications deplete the body's natural balance of nutrients, which must be replaced.

ONE MORE STEP UP

If menopause symptoms remain a problem, it may be appropriate to intervene with what is commonly known as "natural" hormones. While all hormones used as medications must
be transformed in the lab, those labeled "natural" are less
potent than many pharmaceutical hormones because they
resemble the hormones made in a woman's body. They are
available over the counter or from a compounding pharmacy.
The most well-known is "natural progesterone," which is frequently sold in cream form that is rubbed on the skin. Many
women find it relieves hot flashes and helps with breast tenderness, but it may cause breast tenderness in other women.
While less likely to cause depression than synthetic versions
of progesterone, depression remains a potential side-effect.
Dr. Mayo recommends it as a balance to estrogen over the
synthetic version, especially now that it can be prescribed by
a physician and the quality is assured. Compounding phar-
macists can "tweak" hormone formulations to more closely
match a woman's particular needs, and these formulations
may be covered by insurance. Natural hormones are still

hormones and should not be the first line of defense for menopausal symptomology unless lifestyle and botanical interventions have not been effective.

REACHING THE TOP

The very top of our intervention triangle consists of pharmaceutical prescriptions for hormone replacement. The Women's Health Initiative Study (Summer 2002) recommended that women using estrogen/progesterone combinations (HRT) discontinue their use because of increased breast cancer, blood clots, and less-than-expected protective benefits for the heart (one of the main reasons previously given for their use). These combinations are definitely problematic for those with existing heart disease. The study is continuing for women on estrogen (ERT) alone.

Estrogen therapy is beneficial for building strong bones and reducing colon cancer. Several studies indicate it is a preventative against Alzheimer's. Whether or not a woman continues or begins hormone therapy, it must be an informed decision between her and her doctor following a close examination of her baseline health and family history. Currently, the North American Menopause Society and the Association of Obstetricians and Gynecologists recommend that if a woman starts hormones, she should plan on short-term use (3-5 years) for relief of symptoms (depending on her history) during the height of menopausal problems and bone loss. There is no long-term information available on the increasing use of testosterone patches and gels to help alleviate sexual problems or diminished desire.

Because more doctors are hesitant to prescribe traditional HRT, they are recommending their patients try the new "designer hormones" called SERMS (Selective Estrogen Receptor Modulators). While these appear to build bone and in some cases relieve symptoms, they are relatively new and the long-term effects remain unclear. Our recommendation remains that a firm foundation of positive lifestyle interventions is the most important step, and that you move up to hormones as a last resort for uncontrolled symptoms or risks. With each step up the triangle, more potent interventions increase the risk of other health complications.

WHAT TO DO WHEN YOU ARE ALL GROWN UP

With a focus on wellness, our tendency is to consider physical health and to neglect looking at the way we are living our life emotionally and spiritually. One of the greatest things about aging is that it gives us the ability to decide what is important. Unlike other challenges a woman may have faced throughout her life, there is nothing that can be done to stave off aging. Old age must be embraced. In no way does aging signal that she has nothing to offer. The Bible says that the righteous "will still bear fruit in old age; they will stay fresh and green" (Psalm 92:14). Isn't that a wonderful thought? Bearing fruit—ripening well—occurs because living a long time has enabled the acquisition of wisdom, knowledge, and understanding,

What a woman focuses on and how she spends her time becomes more important with increasing awareness that her days are numbered. Examining how we are doing and choosing the good part is in keeping with the mandate of Isaiah 55:2: "Why spend money on what is not bread and your labor on what does not satisfy? Listen, listen to me and eat what is good, and your soul will delight in the richest of fare."

It is good news that an older woman has little energy left for life as usual because it means she has no choice but to prioritize. She has demonstrated resiliency and power throughout her life; now it merely needs to be redirected.

Where does she start? Where do you start? First, examine the balance in your life. Let go of things that are no longer working or that are bogging you down. Eliminate activities that undermine self-confidence, joy, your personal and spiritual growth, and, of course, your health. Ask yourself, "What is meaningful now?" For the first time for most women, direction in life can be defined not by the desires or demands of others, or by what a woman does well based on a lifetime of experience, but rather, on the desires or interests that are ripening within her. The inability to live life as usual is a wake-up call for reevaluation. It requires a concerted effort to change. The fact that there are not endless days ahead gives the process a sense of urgency needed to do what needs to be done and to change what needs to be changed. It is truly "Good News" that you do not have to make the journey alone. "Trust in the LORD with all your heart and lean not on your own understanding; in all your ways acknowledge him, and he will make your paths straight" (Proverbs 3:5–6).

ABOUT THE AUTHORS

Joseph and Mary Ann Mayo have a professional and life partnership. Together they have authored *The Menopause Manager*, have founded A Woman's Place Medical Center, and speak nationally on issues of women's wellness.

Mary Ann Mayo, M.A., M.F.T., is a licensed marriage family therapist who has authored ten books. The latest are *Twilight Travels with Mother* on the fear of getting Alzheimer's and *Good for You! Smart Choices for Balancing Hormones.*

A compassionate practitioner throughout his lifetime, Joseph Mayo, M.D., F.A.C.O.G., completed his obstetrics and gynecology residency at Stanford Medical School and established one of the first medical clinics to focus on the health of midlife women and menopause.

VERSES THAT INSPIRE

Age should speak; advanced years should teach wisdom. (Job 32:7)

[The LORD says,] "Even to your old age and gray hairs I am he, I am he who will sustain you." (Isaiah 46:4)

Children's children are a crown to the aged, and parents are the pride of their children. (Proverbs 17:6)

Many, O LORD my God, are the wonders you have done. The things you planned for us no one can recount to you; were I to speak and tell of them, they would be too many to declare. (Psalm 40:5)

Body Image and Eating Disorders

❧

LINDA S. MINTLE, PH.D.

Do you not know that your body is a temple of the Holy Spirit,
who is in you, whom you have received from God?
You are not your own; you were bought at a price.
Therefore honor God with your body.
—1 CORINTHIANS 6:19–20

Eating disorders, along with negative body image, are serious problems affecting millions of people, especially women. But hundreds of women and men worry about their weight and use food to cope with emotional and relationship issues.

Have you ever made statements like, "I hate my body," "If only I was ten pounds thinner," "When I'm thin I'll be happy," "I can't get control," "I eat when I'm not hungry," "Tomorrow I'll go on a diet," "I have to be thinner than everyone else," or "I feel like throwing up"?

Or maybe you feel the need to be perfect or to always please others. Any mistake means you've failed, and failure is not acceptable. When you fail, you struggle with self-hate.

Or perhaps you are in a destructive relationship, one you know isn't healthy. Or you are secretly angry with your husband but can't bring yourself to tell him because you fear he will leave you.

Unfortunately, the way you cope with these feelings is with food: You binge and then vomit, or you compulsively overeat, or you eat all day and watch the pounds add up. Life just feels out of control!

If any of these descriptions sound like you, you may be at risk for developing an eating disorder. And you are not alone. An estimated 11 million Americans have eating disorders and 34 million are overweight. That's a lot of people struggling with issues around food. So let's try to understand more about eating disorders and food obsession.

FOOD CAN BE ABUSED

Food is easy to abuse because it is cheap, available, tastes good, is physically satisfying, and emotionally comforting. And unlike true addictions, you can't abstain from the abused substance. Because eating is a part of our everyday lives, avoiding it is difficult.

In addition, food abuse does not have the stigma attached to it that alcohol and drug abuse has. Perhaps this explains, in part, why eating problems are so prevalent in the church. Christian activities usually involve food. We meet, greet, and eat in church. You might say food is the acceptable overindulgence used to numb interpersonal and emotional pain. Food can even become an idol and source of obsession. It can be abused by both those with and without faith.

So how does one move from an occasional overindulgence to becoming obsessed with thoughts of food? The answer isn't simple. There are many factors that play into the development of food problems.

WHAT ARE EATING DISORDERS?

Even though they are called *eating disorders*, they aren't just about food. Focusing on dieting and weight may be an obvious beginning to an eating disorder, but much more is involved. Eating habits are disturbed and weight takes on a heightened focus, but the roots of these problems aren't really about food at all.

Most eating disorders emerge around the time of puberty and when a young adult prepares to leave home. These are developmental times of stress because:

- The body is changing
- Sexuality emerges
- Dating relationships begin
- Identity is forming
- Independence increases

Here are some helpful facts to know about eating disorders:

- Eating disorders affect men and women of all ages but are especially seen in young women.
- Eating disorders affect a wide segment of the population, including all social classes, ethnic groups, and races.
- People die from these disorders.
- Early intervention is best.
- Eating disorders are best treated with a multidisciplinary team.

Because eating disorders are primarily a female problem, it is often difficult for males with eating disorders to acknowledge the problem or ask for help. However, the issues underlying food disorders are similar for both sexes, with a few variations for men. Eating disorders in men are often brought on by teasing and taunting by peers and difficulty living up to the masculine ideal. Boys who later develop an eating disorder tend to be non-athletic, and more passive and dependent than boys who do not. Gender identity conflicts and family dynamics play into development as well. All this leads to a negative feeling about the body.

WHAT CAUSES EATING DISORDERS?

The media certainly influences the way women and men feel about their bodies. Americans are bombarded with images of glamour and the perfect body. Everywhere we look, we see bodies sculpted to perfection. Let's face it. Compared to the average model who is 5'8", 100 pounds, and wears a size 2, the average American woman at 5'4", 144 pounds, and a size 12 hardly compares.

There is tremendous pressure in today's world to look beautiful and be thin, but obviously food and weight obsession involves more than these goals or we'd all have eating disorders! Even so, the negative impact of media images cannot be ignored. We now have nine-year-olds dieting, teens requesting plastic surgery, and air-brushed and computer-altered images of glamorous women who appear to be who they are not. Billions of dollars are spent on weight loss products, and for all our efforts, 34 million Americans are still overweight.

While we know that media influences our thoughts and feelings about our bodies, the obvious question is how do an estimated 11 million people go from being somewhat concerned about body and weight to developing eating disorders?

The answer is complex. There is no one factor that causes an eating disorder. A combination of factors is involved. From research and clinical practice, we know that the following factors contribute to the making of an eating disorder:

- Dieting
- History of mood disorders or family history (especially for bulimia)
- Odd family eating habits
- Strong family concern about appearance and weight
- Dissatisfaction with your body and a strong desire to be thin
- Normal developmental events such as puberty, leaving home, a new relationship with the opposite sex
- Repeated negative comments on appearance
- Emphasis on thinness
- Positive family history of eating disorders coupled with dieting
- Personality traits. For example, anorexics tend to be

rigid and perfectionistic. Bulimics often lack impulse control and struggle with unstable moods.

- Family environment
- Possible genetic predisposition

TYPES OF EATING DISORDERS

Anorexia involves severe weight loss (15 percent or more), excessive exercise, food avoidance, distorted body image, fear of gaining weight, and the absence of menses (three consecutive cycles) in women. Medical symptoms such as irritability and depression, gastrointestinal problems, headaches, sensitivity to cold, low pulse and temperature, hair loss, weakness and anxiety, low blood sugar, fainting, and reduced ability to concentrate can result.

Bulimia is characterized by self-induced purging following a binge or compulsive overeating. Purging can take the form of vomiting, laxatives abuse, use of diuretics and/or diet pills, fasting to control weight, or use of ipecac syrup or enemas to rid the body of food. This behavior occurs at least twice a week for three months. Serious medical problems can develop from the binge and purge cycle. They include large weight fluctuations, gastric distress, headaches, skin irritations, electrolyte disturbances, tooth loss and gum disease, depression, and heart failure.

Compulsive Overeating or Binge Eating usually involves impulsive, poorly controlled episodes of binge-eating in which high-calorie foods are consumed in excessive quantities multiple times a day. You eat to the point of feeling uncomfortable and feel disgusted by the way you eat. You may experience chronic and sporadic dieting or fasting, social withdrawal, depression, anxiety and panic attacks, avoidance of school or work, and/or low self-esteem. Because this behavior typically causes weight gain, you may develop medical problems associated with obesity.

RECOVERY OR FREEDOM

Now that you have a basic understanding of the signs and medical complications of these disorders, how do you recover or, better yet, find freedom from such bondage? You need help. Trying to solve this on your own is difficult because you have to learn to connect your eating behavior to the underlying emotions and interpersonal difficulties you experience. For example, do you restrict your eating when you are socially uncomfortable? Do you binge after a fight with your husband? Do you swallow your rejection and hurt by comforting yourself with food? Making the connection between these situations, their accompanying emotions, and your eating behavior is a starting point towards freedom. Eventually you will realize that food is used to cope, numb, and soothe.

Getting better requires that you take a step of faith.

Don't deny the truth. Denial is very common when struggling with an eating disorder. No one likes to admit she has lost control over eating. It signals weakness (though in the case of anorexia, over-control of eating can feel powerful). Denial of the disorder is what stops most people from getting better.

In order to do the necessary work to be free, you must first admit you have a problem. This means letting go of your pride and trusting that people won't hate you or be turned off by your abnormal eating habits. Yes, it is gross to vomit after a meal because you feel stuffed, but hiding this secret will keep you stuck. Facing the truth and acknowledging emotional and spiritual pain is essential. Denial blocks your intimacy with others and God. Getting better requires that you take a step of faith.

Here are other areas of your life to consider when it comes to letting go of the eating symptoms.

- Pride—Usually you need help from God and others around you. Most often a trained mental health therapist and team need to be involved. Put down your pride and get help.

- Control—An eating disorder is a false sense of control. Whether you are out of control or trying to over-control food intake, you've lost control of a healthy eating pattern.

- Deception—Spiritually, don't be deceived by the enemy who wants to destroy you; he can use your eating disorder to destroy your life. Take off the spiritual veil and allow God to work. Your body image will be distorted, so you can't trust what you see in the mirror until you are better. That's why finding a trusted therapist, friends, and family members is important. No one wants you fat. Think about it. No one benefits from you getting fat. God and those who care about you want you well.

- Time—Breaking free from an eating disorder takes time and work. Don't give up when you feel bad or you make mistakes. You must commit to the process. Rarely does someone go from struggle to freedom without taking steps forward and backward. In the end, you will be successful if you don't allow discouragement to overtake you. Give yourself time to make necessary changes.

QUESTIONS TO ASK:

- Will you trust someone to help you?
- Will you be honest about your behavior?
- Will you share your thoughts no matter how stupid or embarrassing they seem?
- Will you face the painful hurts in your life?

- Will you deal with relationship problems and feelings of unworthiness?

- Will you face the deception that you have embraced (such as you are fat, no good, and unlovely)?

- Will you allow God to help you let go of the false control you have and ultimately depend on Him?

- Will you agree to feel uncomfortable in order to get better?

- Will you stop trying to act in your own power?

- Will you tolerate failure?

If your answer is "Yes" to the above, find a trained mental health professional who works with a multidisciplinary team. She will help you develop normal eating habits, establish a healthy weight for your height and body frame, and work on related interpersonal and personal issues.

CONSIDERATIONS FOR TREATMENT

Eating disorders often co-exist with other conditions. You may need to be assessed and evaluated for the following as well. It is not unusual for someone with an eating disorder to also experience depression, anxiety, obsessive compulsive behavior and thoughts, have a history of sexual abuse, or have problems with substance abuse. A therapist can help you deal with these problems as well as the eating symptoms.

The kind of treatment you receive can include everything from going to a support group to being hospitalized. People can die from eating disorders and so, at times, hospitalization may be required. How do you know when? Here are some guidelines:

- Seriously low weight, inability to gain weight
- Can't get control of binge/purge cycle
- Depressed with thoughts of suicide
- Disorganized thinking
- Failure in outpatient treatment

WHAT NEEDS TO CHANGE?

You will need to change your eating habits. That should be obvious. In addition, you must stop dieting, fasting, and compulsive exercising. Stop avoiding certain foods and classifying them into good and bad categories. In addition to changing your eating habits, you will also need to work on your thinking, emotions, identity, sexuality, acceptance, drive for perfection, relaxation, spiritual intimacy, resolution of past hurts, and family and interpersonal relationships.

• *Weight.* Your weight needs to be stable and appropriate for your height and body frame. You may need to work with a registered dietician in order to lose or gain weight. Usually a target (lowest safest weight) and an ideal weight (weight range for your height and body frame) are established. It is important for you to know these weights and work toward these goals no matter how you feel.

• *Renewed thinking.* Your thoughts are powerful influencers of your feelings and behavior. Most people with body image and eating problems have very negative thoughts about themselves. For example, you may think, *I am what I weigh. I have to be thin to be accepted. If people really knew me, they'd hate me.* According to God's Word, you are unique, wonderfully made, and need to have a complete understanding of this and believe it. There are numerous scriptures to learn and upon which to meditate that will strengthen your sense of self. In prayer, ask God to help you understand your strengths and gifts, and know who He is and His promise to never leave you or forsake you. God wants to empower you through His Spirit. He wants you to daily renew your mind through prayer and the reading of His Word. He wants to replace the lies of the enemy with His truths.

You may also need to learn to modify your thoughts. People with eating disorders tend to think in all-or-nothing, black-and-white terms. For example, you may feel unloved when your husband reacts in anger. Instead of thinking, *He doesn't love me,* you must counter those negative all-or-nothing thoughts with more moderate thoughts such as, *Just because he got mad doesn't mean he doesn't love me. Maybe he was having a bad day.*

• *Regulate your emotions.* You must learn to identify what you feel and then regulate those feelings. People with eating disorders often react in extreme ways, either too emotionally or not emotionally at all. A more moderate response is to allow your emotions to surface and not constrict them, or to learn to manage your emotions and not let them manage you. Everyone has to learn to contend with and tolerate bad feelings when they come, not avoid or numb them. Allowing negative feelings to surface is healthy and healing, especially when it involves loss. Learn to identify and express your emotions instead of swallowing them. Then teach yourself to confront those negative feelings in new, assertive ways that incorporate problem-solving methods.

• *True identity.* Eating disorders create false identities. You are not what you eat or defined by your weight. First, find your identity in Christ (you are wonderfully made, created in His image, etc.), and then find your voice and use it. It's scary to assert the real you, but eventually you will be comfortable with this. Allow God to mold you into His image, by His Spirit. He unconditionally loves and accepts you.

• *Sexuality.* Embrace your sexuality. It was created by God and is a beautiful thing. However, like all women, you must learn proper sexual expression and manage your impulses. Don't function in the extremes—either denying your sexuality by starving and staying childlike in body form, or giving in to sexual impulses by being out of control and impulsive.

• *Pleasing others.* Stop giving power to others to determine your worth. Doing and sacrificing for others does not make them love you more. There is a balance between self-care and caring for others that must be learned. The only one you have to please is God. Follow His guidelines for living.

• *Perfection.* Stop trying to be perfect. It's a losing battle filled with anxiety. Only Jesus was perfect. Imperfect people are still loved and accepted by God. In this life, perfection is unattainable. God loves you anyway.

• *Relax.* Many women and girls don't know how to relax their bodies. Practice relaxation strategies and learn the difference between a constant state of tension and relaxation. The more you can relax your body without using food, the better you will feel.

• *Tackle past hurts and relationship issues.* You may need family therapy. Eating disorders are often born from interpersonal pain—a father who was distant, a critical, anxious mother, a sexually abusive uncle, an unpredictable alcoholic father, etc. You must deal with family and interpersonal pain without using food as a coping mechanism. Families help maintain eating disorders because families are often the learning labs for coping with life. Let a therapist help you with needed confrontation, forgiveness, negative family patterns, and interpersonal relationships.

With the help of a therapist, confront past abuse. There is a high correlation between bulimia and sexual abuse. If you were date-raped, experienced marital rape, or were a victim of incest, you need to address this.

If your parents are in an unhappy marriage, it's not your responsibility to fix it. Staying ill may keep them focused on you for a while, but it is not a solution. Let a marital therapist work with them, and you get busy with your own issues around growing up and emotionally leaving home. If you are in an unhealthy marriage, you need to work on the marriage. An eating disorder can be a distraction from the real issues of relationship loneliness and feelings of emptiness. Most likely, you've chosen a partner who is helping to maintain your symptoms. He may want to be the rescuer, or be passive, etc. Whatever the reason, marital work can free both of you from the bondage of these disorders.

You should also address family structure. Usually anorexics come from overly structured families concerned with appearance and looking good at all costs. Bulimics tend to be from more chaotic families that often lack control. The work is to find a middle ground when it comes to family structure.

Here are some family helps:

- Don't promote thinness as great and overweight as horrible.
- Avoid categorizing food into "good" and "bad" foods.
- Respect personal boundaries in the family.
- Avoid negative comments about physical appearance.
- Don't overemphasize body and beauty.

WHERE TO BEGIN

Here's a simple exercise you can begin today to help you better understand why you eat the way you do.

Take a piece of paper and make four columns, labeling them as shown below in the bold type. Then consider the situations, the emotions, and the thoughts that set off a binge or cause you to restrict food, and write them down according to the example below. Over time, you may notice a pattern. Once you see the pattern, you can purpose to these situations, emotions, or thoughts differently (without abusing food).

Situation	Emotion	Thoughts	Behavior
Argued with Husband	Anger	He will leave me	Overate

FREEDOM AND TRANSFORMATION

Recovery is desirable, but freedom is our ultimate aim. You don't have to go through life struggling with food and weight problems. You can be totally free of these disorders as you allow God to move and do the hard work of repair and grieving loss. Nothing is impossible with God. Pray for healing; lose your pride, and work on all the issues we have talked about and you will be set free.

ROOTED IN CHRIST

At the end of this chapter are a number of scriptures to help build your identity in Christ. You are His daughter, and your identity is not dependent on what you do, how much you weigh, or how you look. You are His because of what Christ did for you.

ABOUT THE AUTHOR

Linda S. Mintle, Ph.D., has been a specialist in the field of eating disorders, infertility, and marriage and family issues as a therapist for over twenty years. She was formerly an assistant professor in the Department of Psychiatry at Eastern Virginia Medical School, and is an author, columnist, and commentator.

VERSES THAT INSPIRE

> Then Jesus declared, "I am the bread of life. He who comes to me will never go hungry, and he who believes in me will never be thirsty."
> (John 6:35)

"Can a mother forget the baby at her breast and have no compassion on the child she has borne? Though she may forget, I will not forget you! See, I have engraved you on the palms of my hands." (Isaiah 49:15–16a)

Ah, Sovereign LORD, you have made the heavens and the earth by your great power and outstretched arm. Nothing is too hard for you. (Jeremiah 32:17)

The LORD is my strength and my shield; my heart trusts in him, and I am helped. (Psalm 28:7)

[Jesus said,] "In this world you will have trouble. But take heart! I have overcome the world." (John 16:33)

My God will meet all your needs according to his glorious riches in Christ Jesus. (Philippians 4:19)

Healing from Sexual Abuse

❧

DIANE LANGBERG

My soul is weary with sorrow;
strengthen me according to your word.

—PSALM 119:28

Scripture makes it very clear that there is no evil of which the human heart is not capable (Psalm 140:2), even the evil of sexual abuse. Wonderfully, though, God is a God of redemption. He is more than capable of reaching down to those who have been shattered by sexual abuse and re-creating a life of beauty that brings glory to His name.

WHAT IS SEXUAL ABUSE?

The term "sexual abuse" refers to a wide range of behaviors. It consists of any sexual activity—verbal, visual, or physical —engaged in without consent. Sexual abuse against a child occurs whenever an adult sexually exploits a minor for the satisfaction of the abuser's needs. A child is considered unable to consent due to developmental immaturity and an inability to understand sexual behavior. Sexual abuse against a child is a crime in all fifty states.

Let's consider the various kinds of abuse that might occur. Verbal sexual abuse consists of sexual threats, sexual comments about the child's body, harassment, or lewd remarks. Visual sexual abuse includes such things as pornographic material, exhibitionism, and voyeurism. Physical sexual abuse includes fondling the child's private parts, oral sex, intercourse, or penetration of any kind. Sexual abuse against a minor most often occurs in the context of a relationship where the child has every reason to expect protective care and love from the involved adult. Most sexual abuse is perpetrated by an adult who has ready access to the child by virtue of authority, such as a teacher or youth pastor, or through kinship, such as a parent, uncle, or cousin.

Conservative estimates of childhood sexual abuse in the United States indicate that one in four girls and one in six boys has been molested by the age of eighteen. This can be a one-time occurrence or it can last for years. The average age of the child when the abuse begins is between six and twelve. Studies report that for a smaller percentage, abuse begins before the age of six. We do not know how underreported early abuse might be. Abuse that occurs at a very young age, and that is forceful and repeated, is locked away in the mind and often forgotten for long periods of time. The majority of abusers are male, regardless of the gender of their victims, and most perpetrators are considerably older than their victims.

How Abuse Affects a Woman

The severity of a victim's reaction to sexual abuse depends on many factors. In fact, not all sexual abuse has a long-term impact. Two people can live through similar experiences with quite different responses. Each person is unique.

Several factors contribute to the level of trauma that a victim of sexual abuse feels:

- The more frequently the abuse occurred and the longer the duration
- The more closely related are the victim and the perpetrator
- The wider the age difference between the victim and the perpetrator
- Sexual abuse involving penetration of any kind
- Abuse that is sadistic or violent
- If the victim responded passively or willingly, she will tend to engage in greater self-blame
- If the victim received any negative reaction to an attempted disclosure (such as punishment, accusations, or denial), the effect of the abuse is exacerbated

It is critical, when talking about an adult survivor of childhood abuse, to keep in mind that the abuse occurred as a child and was therefore processed by a child's mind. For this reason, it its beneficial to consider what we know about children:

- Children's knowledge is limited because they have not lived very long.
- Children are vulnerable, dependent, and easily influenced.
- Children also think egocentrically. If you've ever parented a toddler you know that children think the world revolves around them. When parents become divorced, children often believe they are at fault. *If only I had been a good girl, Mommy and Daddy would still be together.* Following sexual abuse, a child might think, *If I were not such a bad girl, this would not be happening. I make people do bad things.*

Additionally, children are in the process of accumulating knowledge. As a child, you are learning how relationships work, differentiating between good and evil, and beginning to discern how to tell the difference between the two. You are beginning to understand truth and lies. You are also coming to understand the difference between male and female, whether you are personally valued, and many other significant concepts. In an abusive situation, children learn that relationships are for using others, good is evil, and evil is good. You learn that being vulnerable or female is bad or dangerous, that pretense is crucial, and that you are trash. Overwhelming lessons such as these are not eliminated when survivors reach adulthood. Rather, such lessons control beliefs for the adult. For all of us, lessons learned throughout childhood provide us with a framework for processing events unfolding today.

The very nature of childhood is an evolving process. Anything that is growing can be shaped. We believe that good nutrition is important for our children because what they consume today affects their health as adults. If we raise children in an environment of love, truth, wisdom, and patience we shape their character in beneficial ways. Conversely, if we raise children in an environment of fear, evil, deceit, and pain we shape their character, but the end result is much different. Gardeners who prune their plants and trees know that shaping something that is young and flexible is far easier than shaping something that is mature, rigid, and possibly misshapen. It is always easier to learn something new as a child rather than as an adult. The effects of ongoing sexual abuse in your life as a child and on your future as an adult can be profound.

What are some of the effects of childhood sexual abuse? As we consider them, it is extremely important to understand that these are *indicators,* not proof. An individual can demonstrate all of these symptoms and yet never have experienced sexual abuse. One effect is that a survivor's relationship with her own body can be unhealthy. Many survivors hate their bodies and engage in self-destructive behavior. Addictions to food, alcohol, sex, and drugs are not unusual. Suicidal thoughts or self-mutilation can occur. Eating disorders and sleep disorders are common. A survivor's emotional life may also be affected, and she may struggle with feelings of anger, fear, depression, and overwhelming grief. Abuse also damages a survivor's thinking, for it has been shaped throughout childhood by lies and deceit.

Childhood sexual abuse involves betrayal, rejection, humiliation, abandonment, and deceit, and so relationships are profoundly affected. For an adult survivor, trust seems impossible, manipulative control may seem necessary, and relationships may be eroded by fear. Thoughts are often filtered through the lies of the abuser, such as "I'm worthless," "God is not good," "Love does not exist," and "No one is trustworthy."

THE SPIRITUAL IMPACT OF ABUSE

Spiritually, the effects of abuse are profound. A distorted image of God coupled with a twisted image of the self creates many barriers to experiencing God's love and grace. God is seen as punitive, capricious, indifferent, or dead. The survivor struggles to comprehend what appear to be two irreconcilable realities: the existence of a caring God and sexual abuse. The mind can acknowledge a caring God and no sexual abuse, or sexual abuse in the absence of a caring God. But how does one reconcile the existence of a loving God and childhood sexual abuse?

Without question, the tentacles of childhood sexual abuse can permeate the life of an adult survivor. Though the severity of the long-term results varies from one individual to the next, such effects are part of the potential outcome of the abuse.

Let's consider a little more closely the spiritual impact of childhood sexual abuse through some true examples of those who experienced such abuse and struggled to understand what they were taught about God in that context. Keep in mind that the abuse happened to a child's mind and heart in a child's body.

Sarah is five. Her parents drop her off at Sunday school every Sunday. She has learned to sing, "Jesus loves me, this I know, for the Bible tells me so. Little ones to Him belong; they are weak but He is strong." Sarah's daddy molests her every week. Sometimes Sarah gets a break because her daddy molests her eight-year-old sister instead. The song she learned says that Jesus loves her and that He is strong. So Sarah asks Jesus to make her daddy stop hurting her. Nothing happens. Maybe Jesus isn't so strong after all, she thinks, or at least not as strong as her daddy. Nothing, not even Jesus can stop her daddy. The people who wrote the Bible and that song must not have known about her daddy. Do you see how this child's beliefs about herself and God might be much different than the truths a nonvictim would hold dear?

Mary is seven. She lives in a house where God is referred to often. But this God seems to have a lot of rules. He says children must do whatever their parents tell them. Mary tries very hard to do what her mommy and daddy say because when she does something wrong, her daddy hurts her and explains that this is how God told daddies to teach little girls to obey. She guesses if you don't do what God says He will also hurt you. So she tries very hard to be good. This example demonstrates a God who is someone to fear because He will punish and hurt anyone who fails to obey. The gift of salvation and grace never enters the picture. Instead, this environment is ripe for producing an unrelenting perfectionist in the adult version of this abused child.

And what might incest teach a little girl about fathers? To these children, fathers are untrustworthy, powerful, and unpredictable, and they inflict pain on those in their care. Fathers betray, abandon, deceive, and abuse. After learning such powerful lessons as a child, how might you feel when someone tells you that God is your Father?

And what does abuse teach a child about God? He's cruel, impotent, uncaring, and if He hears her cries, He does not answer. Children must not be important. He is not who He says He is. He does not keep His Word. Abuse slanders the character of God in the mind of an abused child.

What does abuse teach the child about herself? She is unworthy, unlovable, and her prayers are useless; she is bad and she makes people do bad things. And no matter what she does, nothing brings change or relief.

The following is a story that one survivor wrote as she searched for a way to apply the truth of God's Word to herself and the lies that abuse taught her. This was written by a woman who was abused by her father throughout most of her childhood. She has struggled long and hard with why God didn't stop it. "What was God thinking and feeling," she often asked me, "when my daddy was raping me?" Her story is titled "Mr. Jesus' Abba" and it shows her struggle to see God as a loving Father.

MR. JESUS' ABBA

God doesn't want you to be all filled up with fear.
He is your safe Abba and He will never hurt you.
—ROMANS 8:15 PARAPHRASED

There was once a special little girl named Emma. Emma was a wonderful little girl and Mr. Jesus loved her very much. Emma's daddy didn't love her in safe ways like Mr. Jesus did. Her daddy hurt her sometimes and made her feel like a bad girl. Emma didn't know that not all daddies hurt their little girls. Mr. Jesus knew that Emma's daddy hurt her and that Emma didn't trust daddies anymore. That made Mr. Jesus sad. So Mr. Jesus decided that it was time for Emma to know a safe daddy, His Abba. *Abba* means "safe daddy who loves you without hurting," and that's what Mr. Jesus' Abba is. Mr. Jesus knew that it was important that Emma meet Abba because Emma is His child too. Mr. Jesus' Abba is God and He is everyone's Abba. Mr. Jesus knew that Abba was safe, but Emma didn't. He would have to find a way to make her see that He was a good and loving daddy, not like her daddy who hurt her. So Mr. Jesus showed Emma all about His Abba. He showed her a part of His Book that said, "God doesn't want you to be all filled up with fear. He is your safe Abba and He will never hurt you." Emma thought about that verse and then told Mr. Jesus about how she felt.

"Mr. Jesus," she prayed, "I don't want to know

Your Abba. He's a daddy and that means He's going to hurt me. I don't like that."

Mr. Jesus wasn't angry at Emma for what she said. He knew that she was being honest with Him and telling Him the truth. So Mr. Jesus answered her.

"Emma, I know that you feel very scared of My Abba, but Abba is safe. He's not like daddies you know. He will never hurt you, I promise."

Emma thought about that. She didn't think that daddies were safe, but Mr. Jesus promised her that Abba was safe. Mr. Jesus never broke a promise and Emma knew that. He promised that she could always talk to Him and He kept that promise. He promised that she would never be alone and He kept that promise. Emma had never known a daddy who kept his promise before. But Mr. Jesus always did. So Emma decided to trust Mr. Jesus.

"Mr. Jesus, I'm still kind of scared to meet Your Abba, but I'm going to believe You when You say He's safe. But will you stay right here with me when I meet Him?"

Mr. Jesus smiled, as a tear slipped from his eye.

"Yes, Emma, I'll be right here with you. I'll love you and I'll never leave you. Ever." So Mr. Jesus stood right there with her and they began to talk to Abba.

"Hi, Abba. It's me, Emma. I'm Mr. Jesus' friend."

Abba was happy to hear from Emma. He talked to her in a safe voice. "My precious child, how happy I am to have you here as My daughter. I love you so very much and I've been waiting to hear from you."

Emma saw lots of love in Abba's eyes and she felt safe. She began to talk to her Abba about everything just like she did with Mr. Jesus. Abba was very happy to finally have His little girl with him and Emma was happy to find her loving and safe Abba. She was glad that she believed Mr. Jesus' promise.

Abba is your safe and loving daddy too. He will never hurt you like your daddy did and you can tell Him everything, even that you're scared to talk to Him. He can hardly wait for you to come to Him as His child.

This woman's struggle to come to terms with the truth of who God is versus the lies she was taught as a child clearly demonstrates that childhood abuse can profoundly impact a loving relationship with God, and the resolution of that struggle can take a very long time.

HELPING THE ABUSED WOMAN

Let us suppose you are involved in a women's ministry, a lay counseling group, or a Bible study in your church. At some point, perhaps you are confronted with a woman in her thirties who tells you with great difficulty and hesitation that she was sexually abused by her father for fifteen years. Her mother was aware but never said a word. She has decided to talk to you because she's in crisis, her life is falling apart, and you seem like a safe person to her. She's not sure that her history of sexual abuse has anything to do with her life right now, but she needs to talk to somebody. She has never before shared this with anyone. She is depressed, anxious, and cannot sleep. She has terrible nightmares. She can hardly function. Her husband is upset with her and doesn't understand the problem. In addition, she's finding it very difficult to care for her children. How do you respond?

There are three reactions. First, you can run away because the complexity of the problem is so overwhelming, you don't want to have anything to do with it. A second option is that you can call in an expert and leave quickly but quietly, hoping the expert will help her and you will be happy to greet her at church when she is all better. Or third, you can get down on your knees and ask God to help you assemble the best possible team for this woman—people who will stand by her and walk with her, making sure she gets the help she needs.

Hebrews 13:1–3 tells us, "Keep on loving each other. . . . Remember those in prison as if you were their fellow prisoners, and those who are mistreated as if you yourselves were suffering."

"Keep on loving," it says. Persevere, endure, do not stop. No time limit is set. When you reach out to someone who grew up with chronic sexual abuse, you may be looking at a several-year commitment. They do not heal in a month's time. The rewards will be slow. The consequences of such evil are traumatic and not quickly resolved. We often demonstrate a naive perception of evil when we think in terms of a "quick fix." Hebrews 13:1 also says that we should keep in mind those who are suffering as if we were suffering the identical thing.

As you try to help this traumatized individual, imagine yourself in a similar situation. This woman's mother knew she was being abused, and still the mother did nothing about it. Wouldn't she feel betrayed by her mother, as well? And how might she feel sharing such an ugly story about her family with someone else? What would she be afraid of? What would you think about her now that you know? Maybe she is depressed and sleep deprived. What happens to her mind when she does not get enough sleep? How well do you think she's managing? Is she able to discipline her children effectively? Try to remember a time when you had to function without much sleep. How did you cope? Or what do you think it might be like to get into bed at night utterly exhausted and lie down next to a man, only to have nightmares of your father raping you? How do you suppose she might react to sex with her husband? Might she become so desperate she might try to hurt herself? And how might she feel about men who were in positions of authority, such as a pastor? What do you think the abuse taught her about men

> *An emotionally trauma-tized individual needs someone who will continue to love her as she works through her pain.*

in authority? And what do you suppose this woman believes about God? Do you think she will ever have confidence that God loves and cares for her? Do you think she might even be able to trust you? Hebrews 13 says, *"as if you."* What might you want or need in a similar circumstance?

An emotionally traumatized individual needs someone who will continue to love her as she works through her pain, as well as someone who is trustworthy. Remember, human relationships have been smashed beyond recognition in this woman's life. Trust, hope, and love are foreign concepts to her. God's character, as revealed through a flesh-and-blood friend who remains steadfast, is what this woman needs in order to heal. As women in the body of Christ, are we willing to assume this role for someone who has been abused?

In addition to an enduring friendship, this abused woman will also require help from a professional who treats childhood sexual abuse. You may need to help her find someone. And perhaps you will have to accompany her to the first appointment or two, because it is extremely difficult to sit in the waiting room of a stranger, knowing that you are about to reveal facts that you want to forget.

She may also need practical help. She cannot sleep, she cannot think, and she is not functioning well. Assistance with household chores or with her children might be necessary. Or she may need help so that she can nap in the daytime when nightmares do not rob her of sleep.

Her husband will also require support. He may not understand what his wife is undergoing. He is probably frustrated with her emotional ups and downs, and he may not know how to love her during this time. He will need men in his life who will support him, mentor him, educate him about sexual abuse, and help him learn how to love his wife. He will have to learn how to wait while she heals. Sometimes women who have been abused as children marry men who are also abusive. Her marriage may not be safe, and it may be necessary to question her about her marriage relationship. She will need a friend who will persevere with her, even when she is confused, angry, struggling, and hurting.

BEFRIENDING A SURVIVOR OF ABUSE

When God calls us to walk alongside those who have been abused, part of that call is to be a living example of God's loving character while the woman heals. Jesus came in a bodily form so that you and I might better understand who He is. He also exists in the body of the church, and as part of that body we are called to live in a manner that will reflect His character and grace to others, especially those who need comfort.

With this in mind, let's consider specific guidelines for befriending a survivor of childhood sexual abuse.

1. *Realize that this type of abuse results in deep and enduring consequences.* This is most true when the abuser was a parent, the child was very young, the abuse was chronic, and it was hidden until the child reached adulthood.

2. *Understand the spiritual ramifications if the abuser was a so-called Christian father, mother, uncle, acquaintance, camp*

counselor, or pastor. Beliefs and fears about God, who He is, His love and protection, and His goodness are not easily healed. A few Bible verses will not automatically resolve the longstanding trauma.

3. *Be aware that the survivor will probably want to isolate herself at times.* Being in groups may be difficult. However, strive to keep her connected with those in her support network even if she tries to push them away. But remember that public settings may be overwhelming at times and this is okay. Also, if you tell her to call you when she needs something, you will probably not hear from her. You must initiate and maintain the relationship.

4. *Take any suicide threat seriously.* She needs to notify her counselor or be taken to the emergency room if she is threatening suicide.

5. *Believe what you are told.* Adults do rape and sadistically torture little children. The unimaginable happens.

6. *Remember that healing takes time.* Healing from sexual abuse is not a quick process. Abuse can shatter fundamental beliefs and it takes time to reestablish healthy ones. Our God is indeed a God of redemption, but He usually works it out

through other people. Be patient, and when you feel frustrated, be patient some more.

7. *Reach out as a church community.* Men and women who are in crisis situations often feel isolated and unwanted. The church community can provide a place of support, love, significance, and belonging. Sometimes it's the only family some people possess. Be sure to remember that at holidays and birthdays.

8. *Offer hope without condemnation.* In our darkest hours, we all struggle. Often when someone suffers, they need others to buoy them up with hope and faith. Telling someone who is in crisis to simply "have more faith" will usually increase her despair. It is much better to provide assurance and tell her that you will either pray for her or help her in some practical way.

9. *Try to balance ministry and fun* with a traumatized individual. Often when we reach out to those who suffer, we reduce our relationship with them to pure ministry. The abused woman begins to see herself as a problem to be solved. Include her in pleasurable activities so she feels loved for who she is rather than simply a crisis in need of fixing.

10. *Be a listener.* To listen is to bestow honor on someone. You cannot fix a childhood marred by sexual abuse. A few kind words cannot make it all better. However, you can stand alongside someone while she courageously faces the truth and learns to grow in spite of it. If you are not sure what to say, say nothing, but remain beside her. A loving companion always makes a difficult journey so much easier.

11. *Learn more about the area of struggle in which you are ministering.* If you are going to help someone who is suffering from childhood sexual abuse, read several books on the topic. If you do not understand abuse, you will more than likely inflict more pain.

12. *Help the abused person find a counselor who has expertise in sexual abuse.* Offer to drive your friend to the first appointment.

13. *Never imply that the victim is to blame for the abuse.*

14. *Remember that sexual abuse is a criminal act.* Do not fall into the stereotypical trap of thinking that this was just a dysfunctional family. Sexual abuse is a crime. Children are always to be protected by adults. The abuser carries the responsibility for the crime.

15. *Don't minimize the abuse* by saying things like, "Well, at least you didn't get killed."

16. *Don't probe too far, but don't hesitate to ask questions.* If she does not want to talk, honor her feelings.

17. *Take a long, hard look at your own attitudes.* Walking alongside a survivor of sexual abuse will bring you face to face with your own preconceptions about abuse, sex, good and evil, justice and injustice, women and men.

18. *Recognize the honor that has been bestowed upon you when someone chooses to reveal herself.* To expose a decades-long secret is terrifying. Try to say, "I know it took courage for you to tell me. I believe you, and I consider it a privilege to be the one you chose to tell."

19. *Believe that healing is possible.* As Christians, we know that there is hope and healing in Christ. At the same time, do not be naive. A few truths will not heal this trauma. To greet this kind of tragedy with a few verses or "three steps to healing" is to further damage a person who has been greatly wounded. Such responses are often due to our own discomfort. When we do not know what to say, we often come up with a quick formula so that we feel we have accomplished

something. The consequences of sexual abuse in the formative years is staggering. There is indeed a Redeemer, but again, He usually works through people and over a period of time. Submitting to His process is sometimes as difficult for the person befriending the abused as it is for the survivor.

Having worked for thirty years with men and women who have been sexually abused, I can vouch for two things. First, there is indeed unbelievable evil in this world, directed by an evil prince who brings death and deception, and who leads people to misuse power for their own gratification. The sexual abuse of a child is the work of the enemy. It is a hideous attempt to destroy a life and confuse a mind. Any battle against that enemy will be a fierce one. Survivors of abuse and those who walk with them will find it a difficult war to wage because it deals with truth and lies, life and death, redemption and destruction, hope and despair. Yes, it is a battle about sexual abuse and coping mechanisms, but it is also a battle against the powers of darkness. We cannot do it alone.

Second, there is much work to do. Hard work. Lies must be exposed and truth sought. Death must be traded for life.

Work will need to take place in the body, mind, emotions, relationships, and spirit. It cannot be accomplished in isolation. It requires the help of others—competent, compassionate people who will persevere. But as important as all of this is, it is not enough. You will also need a champion.

Some verses in Isaiah 19 paint a striking picture of this champion. Verses 19 and 20 describe an altar that will be built in honor of God within the borders of Egypt, one of Israel's fiercest oppressors. This altar is a witness to the fact that those who have been oppressed and cried out long and hard to God will be rescued. God will send them a Savior and a champion. An altar to God raised in enemy territory—what a sign of hope, or as Isaiah says, "It will be a sign and witness to the Lord Almighty in the land of Egypt. When they cry out to the LORD because of their oppressors, he will send them a savior and defender, and he will rescue them" (Isaiah 19:20).

If you are someone who has been sexually abused, then you know what it means to live in the midst of an oppressor. Your body and your soul have been abused by an enemy. You have often cried out long and hard, wondering why heaven was silent and uncaring. But your champion, the person of Jesus Christ, was also oppressed and abused, and He knows what you have endured. It is He who is big enough to fight the powers of darkness and the forces of evil. It is He whose power is greater than the power of the enemy. It is He who persevered to the end. I have seen the victory that takes place in the lives of survivors as He has brought beauty to devastated lives, truth in place of lies, and life where death once reigned.

Yes, the battle is hard. It is grueling for you, and to some degree for those who walk alongside you. The work of healing takes longer than we would like. In the midst of it all, when change seems slow and hope is dissipated, the Redeemer speaks. He calls sexual abuse evil and He speaks and teaches truth. In fact, He allowed Himself to be abused and He submitted to death so that we would know that He understands.

As you grapple with these issues yourself or reach out to those in your community who have experienced such abuse, may your work reflect the character of the Redeemer, so that many will have the opportunity to cross the threshold from despair and damage to hope and healing.

ABOUT THE AUTHOR

Diane Langberg is a columnist for *Today's Christian Woman,* an author, and the director of Diane Langberg and Associates. She has written two books on sexual abuse: *Counseling Survivors of Sexual Abuse* and *On the Threshold of Hope: Opening the Door to Healing for Survivors of Sexual Abuse.*

VERSES THAT INSPIRE

Let us then approach the throne of grace with
confidence, so that we may receive mercy and
find grace to help us in our time of need.
(Hebrews 4:16)

[The LORD says,] "As a mother comforts her child,
so will I comfort you." (Isaiah 66:13)

For God has not given us a spirit of fear, but of power and of love and of a sound mind.
(2 Timothy 1:7 NKJV)

[God] is not far from each one of us. "For in him we live and move and have our being."
(Acts 17:27–28)

Then you will call, and the LORD will answer;
you will cry for help, and he will say: Here am I.
(Isaiah 58:9)

[This is what the LORD says—] "Forget the former things; do not dwell on the past. See, I am doing a new thing! Now it springs up; do you not perceive it? I am making a way in the desert and streams in the wasteland." (Isaiah 43:18–19)

Extraordinary Women (EWomen), a ministry of the American Association of Christian Counselors (AACC), is a faith-based movement focused on taking women closer to the heart of God. For more information on our dynamic training programs, conferences, resources, and membership benefits, visit *Ewomen.net* or call 1-800-526-8673 or write P.O. Box 739, Forest, VA 24551.

AACC is a membership organization of more than 50,0000 clinical, pastoral, and lay counselors dedicated to promoting excellence in faith-based counseling. Post Office Box 739, Forest, VA 24551; 1-800-526-8673; *www.aacc.net*

Shine Magazine is a centerpiece publication for Extraordinary Women. *Shine* bridges the gap between a woman's outer and inner beauty. Each issue celebrates the spiritual, intellectual, and physical aspects of womanhood. Isaiah 60:1 "Arise, SHINE, for your light has come, and the glory of the LORD rises upon you."